THE EFFECT OF SCIENTIFIC MANAGEMENT ON THE DEVELOPMENT OF THE STANDARD COST SYSTEM

This is a volume in the Arno Press collection

THE DEVELOPMENT OF CONTEMPORARY ACCOUNTING THOUGHT

See last pages of this volume for a complete list of titles.

THE EFFECT OF SCIENTIFIC MANAGEMENT ON THE DEVELOPMENT OF THE STANDARD COST SYSTEM

Marc Jay Epstein

ARNO PRESS
A New York Times Company
New York • 1978

Editorial Supervision: LUCILLE MAIORCA

First publication 1978 by Arno Press Inc.

THE DEVELOPMENT OF CONTEMPORARY ACCOUNTING THOUGHT
ISBN for complete set: 0-405-10891-5
See last pages of this volume for titles.

Manufactured in the United States of America

Library of Congress Cataloging in Publication Data

Epstein, Marc J
The effect of scientific management on the development of the standard cost system.

(The Development of contemporary accounting thought)
Originally presented as the author's thesis, University of Oregon, 1973.
Bibliography: p.
1. Managerial accounting--History. 2. Cost accounting--History. I. Title. II. Series.
HF5605.E75 1978 657'.42 77-87298
ISBN 0-405-10937-7

THE EFFECT OF SCIENTIFIC MANAGEMENT ON THE DEVELOPMENT OF THE STANDARD COST SYSTEM

by

MARC JAY EPSTEIN

A THESIS

Presented to the Department of Accounting and Quantitative
Methods and the Graduate School of the University of
Oregon in partial fulfillment of the requirements
for the degree of
Doctor of Philosophy

December 1973

Preface

After several years work on this study a proper perspective on its contribution is difficult. The total immersion in the papers of Frederick W. Taylor and early company records was blinding. Now, after many years away from the project at least one perspective may be of interest. The study--the details of the letters, of the journals, of the ledgers--provided tremendous insights for this author. It provided an understanding of the genesis of the field that so many of us devote much of our time to and which we now know as "managerial accounting." That understanding has aided me in both my teaching and my research. Historical research provides us with the necessary perspectives and accounting history research is necessary to further document the development of the discipline . It is my hope that this study will stimulate further research into the area of accounting history generally and managerial accounting history specifically.

Accounting history has already become more widely accepted with increased study, increased research and publications, and the start of an association of accounting historians and a journal devoted to the field. Much more work is necessary if we are to better understand the past and make a linkage to the present and the future.

This publication of my doctoral dissertation is dedicated to one of the most liberal minds in accounting today. Professor Paul Frishkoff was not only chairman of my dissertation committee but also an inspiring teacher. His thoughts, teachings, and writings have always been challenging to the way we view what accounting is and those challenges are what makes accounting the dynamic discipline that it is.

Marc Jay Epstein
Los Angeles, California
February, 1977

VITA

NAME OF AUTHOR: Marc Jay Epstein

PLACE OF BIRTH: Cleveland, Ohio

DATE OF BIRTH: August 24, 1947

UNDERGRADUATE AND GRADUATE SCHOOLS ATTENDED:

San Francisco State College
University of Oregon

DEGREES AWARDED:

Bachelor of Arts, 1968, San Francisco State College
Master of Business Administration, 1970, University of Oregon

AREAS OF SPECIAL INTEREST:

Managerial Accounting
The Measurement of Social Costs
Managerial Planning and Control Systems

PROFESSIONAL EXPERIENCE:

Graduate Teaching Fellow, Department of Accounting and Quantitative Methods, University of Oregon, 1969-1970

Assistant Professor, Department of Accounting, University of Saskatchewan, 1970-1972

Assistant Professor, Department of Accounting, University of Texas at Arlington, 1972-1973

ACKNOWLEDGMENTS

A dissertation is a mammoth undertaking for one person; and I have been fortunate to have had assistance from many people. I would like to express my gratitude to my dissertation committee for their help and suggestions. The committee included Dr. Paul Frishkoff, Dr. Willis Greer, Dr. Dwaine Richins, and Dr. James Tattersall. I would further like to express special thanks to the committee chairman, Dr. Frishkoff. His criticisms and comments were invaluable. His diligent efforts helped see me through to the completion of this dissertation.

I would also like to thank my wife. Without Joanne's constant prodding, persistent help, and constant moral support, this dissertation would not be completed today.

A gracious thank you goes to Georgia Leshikar who labored so hard at typing the various stages of this study.

Of course, any errors remain my responsibility.

TABLE OF CONTENTS

LIST OF EXHIBITS

CHAPTER I

INTRODUCTION

> Accounting history is the study of the evolution in accounting thought, practices, and institutions in response to changes in the environment and societal needs.[1]

Accounting history, as an academic discipline, has been a neglected area of study. In contrast with most other disciplines, little study has been made of the development, progress, and change of the discipline over time. One explanation for this is that there is simply not enough accounting history to report. A more reasonable explanation, I think, is that though accounting is not new, its development as an area of scholarly pursuit is recent. It only became an academic discipline when it changed from its "technical" or vocational orientation. According to William Morse Cole, as of 1898 "no college in the country then offered any course in accounting as a part of its academic work."[2] Perhaps most significantly, many accounting researchers think that accounting history is not very interesting. With accounting

---

[1]American Accounting Association, Report of the Committee on Accounting History, Accounting Review, Supplement to Volume XLV, 1970, p. 53.

[2]W.M. Cole, "The Rise of Accountancy," The Journal of Accountancy, Vol. VII, No. 4 (February, 1909), p. 295.

techniques advancing in sophistication at a rapid rate, many people feel that studying methods of five or fifty years ago is not worthwhile. Whatever the reason, the result of the lack of study of accounting history is that "the field is not organized and developed academically to the same degree as are the historical aspects of other disciplines."[3]

Relationship Between Scientific Management and Cost Accounting

One of the more interesting aspects of accounting history has been the relationship of the development of cost accounting to the development of scientific management. Many writers submit to the validity of this relationship but no scholarly research has documented any connection.

Though this will be further discussed at a later point, it should be noted here that the mechanical engineers, as mainly evidenced through their meetings reported in the Transactions of the American Society of Mechanical Engineers, were at the forefront of establishing new cost accounting methods in the companies where they worked.

---

[3]Richard H. Hamburger, "Sources of Accounting History," An appendix to the Report of the American Accounting Association's Committee on Accounting History, Accounting Review, Supplement to Vol. XLV (1970), p. 64.

> It was largely due to the mechanical engineers that by 1901 progress had been made in the elaboration of methods for the handling of overhead costs, for instance, and for their rationalization. Accounting historians, who provided masterly studies of the growth of their discipline, discern occasional comments which they interpret as the germ of the ideas of 'standard' or 'predetermined' costs, which have come in recent decades to dominate advanced thinking in the field. Certainly such leading practioners as Taylor and Emerson were computing standard costs by 1910, but neither had made clear in public just how the concept and its implications were to be worked out in practice.
>
> What is certain is that the development of cost accounting practice as distinct from doctrine, depended upon the rise of standardized shop conditions.[4]

One of the primary duties of the engineer in his company during the period was to standardize and systematize the company operations so that they were able to earn maximum profits for the owner. The engineers realized that essential to higher profits was a better method of establishing and estimating costs in accord with more standardized shop conditions. Since accountants mainly concerned themselves with "cost-keeping" during this time, the burden was on the engineers to develop these new techniques.[5]

---

[4]Leland H. Jenks, "Early Phases of the Management Movement," Administrative Science Quarterly, Vol. V (December, 1960), p. 434.

[5]Cost-Keeping activities are being distinguished here from cost-finding activities. Cost-keeping is being defined as those activities concerned primarily with the recording and classification of actual manufacturing costs for purposes of financial statement preparation. Cost-finding is being defined as those activities concerned primarily with the determination of actual product costs to aid in cost control and overall managerial decision-making. These activities are to be further distinguished from the more advanced methods involved in standard cost systems.

This relationship between standard cost accounting and scientific management is again briefly discussed in the Industrial Accountants Handbook, which serves as a guide for practicing cost accountants.

> Historically speaking, standards for management control and cost purposes may be said to have been developed and applied in a practical way by the late Dr. Frederick W. Taylor, who is regarded generally as the father of scientific management. In a larger sense, standards have been used consciously or unconsciously in every industrial and business establishment since commerce and industry began. But Dr. Taylor seems to have been the first to apply the fundamentals of the use of standards and provide (1) a carefully thought out method of performing a task, (2) a fair standard time for performing the task, (3) a means of controlling actual results and comparing them with this predetermined task, and (4) a plan for rewarding those who exceeded the standards. As business increased in complexity and industrial organizations expanded and grew in size, the need of some means of measuring performance and providing control over operations became increasingly recognized. As a result, the use of standards for management and cost purposes has expanded greatly, and in various stages of development standards appear in every industry.[6]

Need for the Study

Thus, though many have briefly noted that a relationship between scientific management and the development of the standard cost system exists, it has yet to be proven. A need exists to further develop the historical aspects of accounting generally

---

[6] John A. Beckett, ed., Industrial Accountants Handbook (Englewood Cliffs, New Jersey: Prentice-Hall, Inc., 1964), p. 243.

and the basis and development of managerial accounting specifically.[7] Many recommendations have been made for a study of the evolution of the standard cost system. The most recent suggestion of this was by the American Accounting Association's Committee on Accounting History when it suggested the "effects of the 'scientific management' movement on the evolution of standard cost accounting" as a needed research topic.[8] It suggested that such historical research "is a continuing and necessary element in the overall research effort of scholars in an academic discipline."[9] Managerial accounting history, particularly, has been neglected. Just as double-entry bookkeeping is the basis of our currently used financial accounting system, the standard cost concept is the basis of our currently used managerial accounting system. Thus, just as the study of the development of double-entry bookkeeping is of great interest to financial accountants, the development of the standard cost system

---

[7]Managerial or management accounting is defined here as the preparation of financial information for internal or management decision-making. This is distinguished here from the more specific term of cost accounting which will refer to the determination and reporting of product costs. These terms are further distinguished from financial accounting which is defined here as the preparation of financial information for external decision-making. It should be noted that the terms managerial accounting and cost accounting are often used interchangeably.

[8]American Accounting Association, p. 53.

[9]American Accounting Association, p. 55.

should be of great interest to managerial accountants. Further, an understanding of the beginnings and development of managerial accounting should provide for a better understanding of the status of managerial accounting today.

This thesis will attempt to prove

1) that the scientific management movement had an important and direct effect on the development of the standard cost system, and

2) that this effect was caused by the requirements of scientific management in its application in industry.

Some Important Definitions

Scientific management is a system that attempts to increase worker efficiency by setting standards for: the worker, the quality of his equipment, and the methods of doing work. The basis of this system is elementary time study. Each phase or operation in the work process is timed to determine a standard of how much workers can be expected to produce. Wage rates are then set accordingly. Scientific management attempts, as much as possible, to standardize all industrial operations.

> Scientific management . . . has for its very foundation the firm conviction that . . . prosperity for the employer cannot exist through a long term of years unless it is accompanied by prosperity for the employee, and vice versa; and that it is possible to give the workman what he wants most--high wages--and the employer what he wants--a low labor cost--for his manufactures.[10]

---

[10]Frederick Winslow Taylor, The Principles of Scientific Management (New York: Harper and Brothers Publishers), p. 10.

Scientific management necessitated a new kind of accounting system that could break down production costs into the various component parts and estimate them for future production. It needed an accounting system that could determine actual costs and compare those costs with the predetermined standards that the engineers had arrived at. It needed an accounting system that could attach costs to these predetermined standards of performance. These requirements for the system of scientific management made it necessary for both engineers and accountants to attempt to develop ways of providing this information. Standard cost accounting was that development.

Standard cost accounting has been defined many different ways by many different authors. Essential to these definitions is the comparison of actual costs with the predetermined or estimated costs. In A Dictionary for Accountants, standard costs are defined as:

> a forecast or predetermination of what costs should be under projected conditions, serving as a basis of cost control and as a measure of productive efficiency when ultimately compared with actual costs. . . .A standard-cost system lays stress upon exceptions and permits concentration upon inefficiencies and other conditions that call for remedy.[11]

---

[11]Eric L. Kohler, A Dictionary for Accountants (Englewood Cliffs, New Jersey: Prentice-Hall, Inc., 1963), 3rd edition, p. 456.

Kohler is here discussing the concept of variances and variance analysis that is an integral part of any standard cost system. These exceptions or variances will become significant as the development of the standard cost system is traced.

Kohler also indicates that this concept of a standard cost is

> a product of the scientific management movement. The leaders in this movement stressed improvements in manufacturing methods and the embodiment of approved methods in standards which could serve both as goals toward which to work and as measures of performance.[12]

The creation of standards links these two systems. When the concepts of scientific management began to gain recognition among factory owners, there were no adequate accounting systems that could record this kind of data. Alexander H. Church wrote in 1900: ". . . the majority of firms of any size have some sort of cost method, however rough and home-made, which enables them to tell how much labour and what value of material have been expended on any particular job."[13] Church is speaking here of a cost keeping system, where actual costs were accounted for. He later indicates the need for a better accounting system that would include the important concept of standards established by the scientific management movement.[14]

---

[12] *Ibid*., p. 457.

[13] Alexander H. Church, "The Meaning of Commercial Organization," *Engineering Magazine*, Vol. XX, No. 3 (December, 1900), p. 394.

[14] *Ibid*., p. 397.

Review of the Management Literature

Before proceeding with the development of scientific management, two recent important works on the scientific management movement should be noted. Sudhir Kakar wrote a psycho-historical study on F.W. Taylor, the acknowledged "father of scientific management." In this book,[15] Kakar shows the relationship between Taylor's personal conflicts and the development of his system of scientific management.

> From this conflict also stems, according to Professor Kakar, the nature of his management theories: his fanatical search for the 'one best way' to perform every task, his unilateral definitions of 'a fair day's work for a fair day's pay,' his anti-unionism, and his unwillingness to let the rank and file workers do any thinking for themselves.[16]

There is some question among historians as to the validity of psycho-historical research, since it relies so heavily on inference rather than on a factual base. This study is important, though, in that it indicates the motivational and causal base for the development of scientific management. More important, for

---

[15]Sudhir Kakar, Frederick Taylor: A Study in Personality and Innovation (Cambridge, Mass: MIT Press, 1970).

[16]"Book review of Sudhir Kakar's Frederick Taylor: A Study in Personality and Innovation," Management Services (January-February, 1971), p. 58.

this study, it also indicates why standards were such an important facet of Taylor's system.

Samuel Haber in Efficiency and Uplift, makes a significant contribution by placing the scientific management movement in the context of the era in which it developed, 1890-1920. The Progressive era gave rise to an efficiency craze which was preached by all facets of American society--doctors, housewives, teachers, businessmen, and preachers. At the center of this was F.W. Taylor and his scientific management movement. Haber found that "scientific management can serve as a tracer element to reveal some of the less familiar aspects of the vast movement for progressive reform."[17] In his study he looks at the relationship of the scientific management movement to the reformers of the Progressive era.

There have been some earlier references of systems that seem similar in many ways to that of Taylor's. These systems, though poorly documented and described, are only isolated instances of sophistication in the planning of efficient systems of production. As can be seen throughout the history of financial accounting, the isolated instances are not the causes of new major changes in practices. It is, instead, the spreading of the information that causes the change.

---

[17]Samuel Haber, Efficiency and Uplift: Scientific Management in the Progressive Era, 1890-1920 (Chicago: University of Chicago Press, 1964), p. ix.

One excellent example of this early sophistication in manufacturing, management and accounting techniques is the Soho Foundry of Boulton and Watt. Their first partnership began in 1775 as consulting engineers, rather than as manufacturers of steam engines.

> They made it clear in their answers to all the early inquiries that all they were prepared to do was to furnish suitable plans and drawings, and supervise the erection of the engine, while the customer would be at liberty to have the engine parts made wherever he chose.[18]

The first need for standardization came in 1780 when Boulton saw a need for the manufacture of spare parts "for stock in order to reduce the delay which the replacement of broken parts usually involved."[19] This necessitated, at least, standardization of spare parts and eventually in 1782, led to the recognition that standardization of the engine itself was essential.

In fact it was not until 1795 that the Soho Foundry was built and the company began to manufacture steam engines. "It was not James Watt, senior and Matthew Boulton who were responsible for the details of the management of Soho Foundry," but their sons James Watt, Jr. and Matthew Robinson Boulton who "brought to the

---

[18]Sir Eric Roll, An Early Experiment in Industrial Organisation (London: Frank Cass and Company, Ltd., 1930), p. 24.

[19]N.S.B. Gras and Henrietta Larson, Casebook in American Business History (New York: Appleton-Century-Crofts, Inc., 1939), p. 20.

business an intelligence and a capacity which are ordinarily associated only with modern scientifically trained business managers."[20]

In his chapter on scientific organization in which elementary scientific management concepts are discussed, Roll states that "the years 1800 and 1801 mark not only a turning point in the planning of extensions at Soho, but appear to provide also the earliest records in existence of systematic factory planning."[21] In a paper entitled, "Arrangement of the Engine Manufactory, Soho, Dec., 1801,"[22] a list of shops and their operations are conveyed in primitive form. In the appendix we also find a schedule for ascertaining piece rates,[23] a chart for standardized parts and a primitive time study.[24]

Wages were paid on a piece rate system whenever possible, and "where piece rates could not be set satisfactorily, the firm introduced the granting of 'gratuities' or bonus additions to the daily wage, based on the amount of work finished."[25]

---

[20]Roll, Early Experiment, p. xv.

[21]Ibid., p. 169.

[22]Ibid., See plates, p. 316.

[23]Ibid., Appendix XIV, p. 307.

[24]Ibid., Appendix XVI, p. 309.

[25]Gras and Larson, American Business History, p. 297.

We can clearly see some basic scientific management concepts throughout Boulton and Watts' factory. The mere fact, though, that their system did not become well-known and duplicated in other factories of the time, allows us to conclude that scientific management was still a dormant concept yet to be awakened by F.W. Taylor and associates. It cannot be proven that standard cost concepts originated first with the development of scientific management around the turn of the twentieth century partly because isolated instances could have occurred earlier in history. But, most important is that the standard cost system had not been widely used, written about, or implemented in the United States. The example of Boulton and Watt could be just one example of many isolated instances of advanced management and accounting practices throughout history, but it was not until the development and spread of Frederick Winslow Taylor's concept of scientific management that a complete and widely used standard cost system was developed.

The foundations upon which managerial accounting has developed have never been thoroughly discussed. Although Solomons, Weber, Parker and Jenks all acknowledge the close connection between standard costing and the scientific management movement, no one has ever systematically attempted to prove any significant cause-effect relationship.

Review of the Accounting Literature

A brief review of accounting history work already done, will show both the lack of, and the need for, more in depth studies. Much of the writing in accounting history has been concerned with the origins of double-entry bookkeeping and the development of financial accounting. Significant contributions have been made by Raymond de Roover, A.C. Littleton, and Basil Yamey, Richard Brown, Wilmer Green, Michael Chatfield and others.[26] Though the treatment of financial accounting history is less than adequate, it is in the area of managerial accounting history that the least amount of research has been completed.

Research in the history of managerial accounting has been small. Most well-known of the research is: S. Paul Garner's, Cost Accounting to 1925.[27] In the preface to his book, Garner

---

[26]See Raymond de Roover, "Aux origines d'une technique intellectuelle: La formation et l'expansion de la compatabilité à partie double," Annales D'histoire Économique et Sociale, Vol. IX (1937), pp. 171-93, 270-98; A.C. Littleton, Accounting Evolution to 1900 (New York: American Institute Publishing Company, 1933); A.C. Littleton and B.S. Yamey, eds., Studies in the History of Accounting (London: Sweet and Maxwell, 1956); Richard Brown, A History of Accounting and Accountants (New York: Augustus M. Kelley, 1905); Wilmer L. Green, History and Survey of Accountancy (Brooklyn: Standard Text Press, 1930); and Michael Chatfield, Contemporary Studies in the Evolution of Accounting Thought (Belmont, California: Dickenson Publishing Company, Inc., 1968).

[27]S. Paul Garner, Cost Accounting to 1925 (Univ., Ala.: University of Alabama Press, 1954).

clearly indicates that the focus is on actual costs rather than standard costs.

> The cost accounting practices considered in this study are for the most part those concerned with the ascertainment of the so-called actual (accounting) cost of production. More specifically, the line of demarcation is drawn so as to include a rather comprehensive discussion of the following topics: the accounting for raw material, direct labor, and manufacturing burden (from several aspects), the question of the integration or non-integration of the factory and financial accounts, the accounting for interdepartmental transfers of product, the costing of by-products and co-products, the handling of waste materials and scrap, the development of job order and process cost systems and the problem of valuing factory inventories.[28]

He isolates each area and then develops them chronologically with a great deal of detail. He has done an extensive literature search and seems to include most of the accounting literature to 1925.

His treatment of the historical development of standard cost accounting is very limited and scattered throughout the book. He acknowledges this fact by explaining that the book is not a history of standard cost accounting and indicates that "this aspect of accounting evolution deserves a separate volume."[29]

For example, in a section of Garner's book dealing with the manufacturing burden, he adds a brief passage on standard cost accounting development. He says:

---

[28] *Ibid.*, p. ix.

[29] *Ibid.*, p. x.

> In the United States the trend seemed more and more towards the normal predetermined burden rate plan. Several authorities advocated its use in the early 1920's sometimes with a slight modification, but generally about the same. The practice gradually worked into complete standard costing systems. More and more attention began to be given also to the determination of the normal percentage of capacity and all the attendant problems connected therewith.[30]

Though he refers to standard costing, his treatment is by no means comprehensive. He does not discuss the origin or the development of standard costing in any detail.

Garner includes both English and American cost accounting techniques. He reasons that English cost accountants made significant contributions in both technique and theory in the years prior to 1900, which was before the significant American contributions began. He answers the question of how early cost accounting developed, but not why it developed. One of the objectives of my study will be to attempt to explain some of the reasons why cost accounting developed the way it did.

In addition to Garner, others have written books and articles on the history of managerial accounting. Of these, David Solomons, Karl Weber, and R.H. Parker are also of major importance.

---

[30] *Ibid.*, p. 243.

David Solomons' "The Historical Development of Costing"[31] briefly traces the main developments in the use of accounting in industry and agriculture from the middle ages to 1950. Solomons states that the costing renaissance began in the late 1880's, and still continues. In this period he states three main lines of development away from "actual cost" to "standard cost" as follows:

> 1. Refinements in the apportionment of overheads were introduced in an endeavour to make the cost records more accurately reflect the facts of the situation.
>
> 2. Methods were devised to isolate the effect on costs of changes in the scale of output, so that the effect of changes in other factors could be detected, while at the same time breaking the vicious circle of contracting demand and increasing unit costs.
>
> 3. Finally, a technique was developed to separate out and quantify the effect of all significant changes in the factors which determine costs.[32]

Solomons' work is important as a beginning inquiry into the development of cost accounting. Though he does not develop the integration of standard costs into accounting techniques, nor the importance of its relationship to scientific management, he briefly mentions this relationship:

> It is impossible to take any discussion of the origins of standard costing far without acknowledging its close connection with the 'scientific management' movement in America generally, for standard costs mean little without

---

[31] David Solomons, "The Historical Development of Costing," in David Solomons, ed., Studies in Cost Analysis (Homewood, Illinois: Richard D. Irwin, Inc., 1968), pp. 3-50. First printed in David Solomons, ed., Studies in Costing (London: Sweet and Maxwell, 1952).

[32] Ibid., p. 20.

> standard processes and standard operating times, such as F.W. Taylor and his followers developed. No one can read Taylor's famous paper on "Shop Management" of 1903 without seeing that many of the essential elements of standard costing are there, including what is perhaps the first reference to 'management by exception.'[33]

Amerikanische Standardkostenrechung: Ein Überlick, a very important work by Karl Weber, includes two chapters on the historical aspects of standard cost accounting prior to 1920. The work has had little, if any, reference in previous studies primarily due to the fact that there are no known translations.[34]

Though excellent in many respects, Weber's treatment of the historical development is inadequate. He relies heavily on Solomons' paper but, as is true with Solomons, he does not treat the historical aspects of managerial accounting with the thoroughness needed.[35]

In Management Accounting: An Historical Perspective, R.H. Parker discusses the development of accounting as an aid to decision making. He prefaces his book by stating that;

---

[33]Ibid., p. 37.

[34]The title, as translated, is American Standard Cost Accounting: An Overview. No translations were uncovered during the literature search, and a discussion with Professor Adolph Matz of the University of Pennsylvania on January 2, 1973, indicated that there were no known translations. Matz is a close friend of Weber's and author of the preface of the book.

[35]Karl Weber, Amerikanische Standardkostenrechung: Ein Überlick (Varlag P.G. Keller - Winterthur, 1960).

All references to Weber's text will be to an unpublished personal translation by Joanne McKnight.

> accountants cannot claim to be the originators of either the underlying concepts or the practical techniques. In general, economists have been responsible for the concepts and engineers for the techniques.[36]

In the first part of the book he discusses the development of cost concepts for decision-making, discounted cash flow, and the origins of the break even chart. The second part of the book gives the most complete, to date, bibliography of accounting history. He follows this with a chronology of accounting from 1130 to 1966 within the economic and political environments. Though very brief, Parker has presented a useful survey of significant developments in the history of managerial accounting. But, his work and the work of the others mentioned here (especially Garner) demonstrate the need for a comprehensive look at the origins of the standard cost system.

Organization of this Study

With this review of the literature, the need for this study should be apparent. Chapter II will discuss the research methodology employed. It will also give the reader a feeling for the historical setting during which scientific management and standard cost account-

---

[36]R.H. Parker, Management Accounting: An Historical Perspective (London: Macmillan and Company, Ltd., 1969), p. 11.
The reader should note here that the contention that the engineers have been responsible for the underlying techniques of standard cost accounting will be a major aspect of this thesis.

ing grew. Chapters III and IV will then outline the historical development of scientific management and the accounting concepts preceeding standard costs. Then, through an analysis of relevant literature of the period in Chapter V and an analysis of scientific management case studies in Chapter VI, this study will show the effect of scientific management on the development of the standard cost system.

CHAPTER II

METHODOLOGY AND HISTORICAL SETTING

The Historical Method

The title of Edward Carr's book, What is History? is an important question to be considered before the methodology of historical research can be understood. R.G. Collingwood's writing on the philosophy of history and how it has evolved until the "present day," devotes some time to the definition of history; its nature, object and processes.[1] He concludes that:

> Historians nowadays think that history should be (a) a science, or an answering of questions; (b) concerned with human actions in the past; (c) pursued by interpretation of evidence; and (d) for the sake of human self-knowledge.[2]

This definition, by one of the most respected philosophers of history, has important implications for historical inquiry. History can be considered a science, in that it deals with the asking and answering of questions. Scientific methods essentially begin by asking a question. In pure science the question can be answered through direct observation by the scientist. Thus, when

---

[1]R.G. Collingwood, The Idea of History (London: Oxford University Press, 1946), ("Present day" implies up to the time of Collingwood's passing in 1943.)

[2]Ibid., pp. 10-11.

we question how long the life cycle of amoebae are, we can observe this phenomenon through our microscope and measure it with clocks and stop watches. On the other hand, history, being of the past, does not permit direct observation. So, historical events are studied "inferentially, arguing them from something else which is accessible to our observation, and which the historian calls 'evidence' for the events in which he is interested."[3] By inference, the historian claims knowledge by exhibiting the grounds upon which the knowledge is based.

Collingwood warns us about using "testimony" as evidence.

> When the historian accepts a ready-made answer to some question he has asked, given him by another person, this other person is called his 'authority,' and the statement made by such an authority and accepted by the historian is called 'testimony.' In so far as an historian accepts the testimony of an authority and treats it as historical truth, he obviously forfeits the name of historian; but we have no other name by which to call him.[4]

Collingwood does not maintain that testimony ought never to be accepted. "When testimony is reinforced by evidence, our acceptance of it is no longer the acceptance of testimony as such; it is the affirmation of something based upon evidence, that is, historical knowledge."[5]

---

[3] *Ibid.*, pp. 251-52.

[4] *Ibid.*, p. 256.

[5] *Ibid.*, p. 257.

In this thesis, I have attempted wherever possible to go to primary resource material, to base conclusions on evidence rather than to rely on authorities.

Collingwood sees a mutual relationship between the historian and the history he studies. An historian studies the past, which can become meaningful only when he understands the thought behind the history. Thus,

> all history is the history of thought, and history is the re-enactment in the historian's mind of the thought whose history he is studying. The reconstitution of the past in the historian's mind is dependent on empirical evidence.[6]

Thus, the interpretation of facts by the historian is what makes them historical facts.

One of the dangers of Collingwood's philosophy of history is its

> emphasis on the role of the historian in the making of history. If pressed to its logical conclusion, to rule out any objective history at all: history is what the historian makes.[7]

Edward Carr, on the other hand, feels that the obligation of the historian is to seek "all known or knowable facts relevant, in one sense or another, to the theme on which he is engaged and to the interpretation proposed."[8]

---

[6]Edward H. Carr, What is History? (New York: Alfred A. Knopf, 1962), p. 24.

[7]Ibid., p. 29.

[8]Ibid., p. 32.

We can then conclude that history "is a continuous process of interaction between the historian and his facts, an unending dialogue between the present and the past."[9]

Libraries and Periodical Literature Searched

Acting as an historian, I have attempted to "seek out" all facts relevant to this thesis, through an exhaustive literature search. In June, 1971, and again in December, 1972, I conducted research at the F.W. Taylor Collection of the Stevens Institute of Technology in Hoboken, New Jersey. One of the difficulties in historical research is the problem of locating all relevant materials. The Taylor Collection is, in many respects, poorly organized and not well maintained. But, many valuable items that seem to have never before been thoroughly examined and organized were discovered. This collection of Taylor's life-long work is quite inclusive. There are documents relating to his correspondence through the years, his patents, his relations with various universities and societies that gave him honor, and all of his work in the field of scientific management. The collection includes a wealth of primary resource material pertaining to the installation of scientific management, as a system, in various business concerns. (A list of these businesses is included as Appendix A.)

---

[9]*Ibid.*, p. 35.

Numerous accounting forms, manuscripts and letters dealing with the companies he served and directly related to the standard cost system were discovered after extensive research in Hoboken. Newspaper clippings about scientific management were also extremely helpful in gaining a better perspective of the scientific management movement in its time.

In addition, libraries such as the American Institute of Certified Public Accountants' Library in New York, New York University's Graduate School of Business library, the New York Public Library, Columbia University's Baker Library, and the U.C.L.A. Research Library were searched for relevant material. All of these libraries have relatively large collections of business history.

The main professional organization in which scientific management had its birth, and in which standard cost accounting developed was the American Society of Mechanical Engineers. F.W. Taylor was president of this society from 1906-1907. All issues of the _Transactions of the American Society of Mechanical Engineers_ were thoroughly searched for relevant material. These volumes dated from 1880 onward. Also, all issues of the proceedings of the _Meetings of the Taylor Society_ (1914-1935) were reviewed.

Among the accounting journals, _The Journal of Accountancy_ offered the most insight into the state of accounting from

1905-1920.[10] There were extensive discussions on such items as:

(1) whether or not to include items such as interest and rent in the calculation of manufacturing cost and

(2) the proper method for the distribution of the expense burden (overhead).

Although these discussions are pertinent to cost accounting generally, they do not deal with the creation of standards and the comparison of those standards with actual performance.

The Accountant, an English journal, was also thoroughly searched. Numerous articles pertaining to scientific management and cost accounting in Great Britain were found though these are not being used extensively in this thesis. Although English accountancy is important, the necessity of limiting this study to the United States was essential in light of the voluminous material. In addition, little connection could be found between English and American accounting during this era of 1890-1920. Finally, the link between the development of scientific management in the United States and the move towards standardization in England is weak at best. One explanation seems to be that the lengthy travel periods for correspondence and travel across the Atlantic Ocean limited the flow of information among management and accounting writers between these two countries.

---

[10]The first issue of The Journal of Accountancy was published in November, 1905, by the American Association of Public Accountants under the editorship of Joseph French Johnson and Edward S. Meade.

Other accounting journals such as The Accounting Review, The National Association of Accountants' Yearbook, and the Journal of Accounting Research were searched with some material being found.

Of special interest was the Business History Review, which contained many articles placing the scientific management movement in the context of the entire history of business during the period under study.

Hypothesis and Methodology Employed

The hypothesis of this thesis, that the scientific management movement had an important effect on the development of the standard cost system, will be proved by two methods.

(1) The first method used is an attempt to demonstrate the effect of the development of scientific management on standard cost accounting through an exhaustive search of the literature of the time. Professional, academic, and popular journals are used to trace the development of standard costing. In addition, unpublished manuscripts are used to further document this development. Standard cost accounting systems were seldom discussed in the journals until 1911. The popularization of scientific management can be attributed

directly to the Eastern Rate Case[11] in November, 1910. Prior to these hearings, few, if any, articles whose title included "scientific management" had been published. During 1911 and 1912, though, forty articles appeared in which "scientific management" was incorporated in the title.[12] The Eastern Rate Case brought the elements of scientific management to the attention of writers who began writing articles and books pertaining to scientific management for both professional audiences and the general public. As previously stated, it is the popularization and spread of scientific management that is more important than the first development. I maintain that this popularization is due in large part to the writings in the newspapers and journals, and that this popularization and development of both scientific management and standard costing can be seen through a careful search of the literature.

---

[11]In this case, the railroads attempted to obtain approval from the Interstate Commerce Commission for an increase in shipping rates. The companies felt that this was necessary due to increases in their operating costs, which were a direct result of wage increases. Those opposed to these rate increases, the Eastern shippers, hired Louis D. Brandeis to defend them in court. Brandeis called experts on scientific management to testify that the railroads could decrease their operating costs by as much as $1,000,000 a day by using scientific management techniques. This received much newspaper coverage and introduced scientific management to the people in the United States.

[12]See H.B. Meyer, "Select List of References on Scientific Management and Efficiency," <u>Efficiency Number of Special Libraries</u>, Library of Congress, May, 1913.

(2) The second method that will be used to demonstrate the effect of scientific management on the development of the standard cost system is the case method. As stated previously, many companies "installed" the Taylor system in their businesses. Through an analysis of the existing documents (accounting forms, correspondence, and reports), it will be shown that a standard cost accounting system was an integral part of the Taylor system. For scientific management to succeed, a better system for the collection and recording of data concerning the actual costs of production and the costs incurred if production was at the level of the predetermined standard was needed. The Taylor Collection includes numerous documents, never before published, nor previously referred to, which help to demonstrate that relationship. Selected cases will be used to show how standard costing was first developed and integrated into the Taylor system. With these two methods of research, the effect of scientific management on the development of the standard cost system will be evident.

In an attempt to discover even more complete information about the companies to be discussed than is available in the Taylor Collection, letters were sent to all companies presently in existence that used the Taylor system. No useful information was obtained. (Three examples of responses have been included as Appendix B.)

The thesis has been divided up chronologically into three time periods:

1. 1875 - 1900
2. 1900 - 1910
3. 1910 - 1920

A study of both accounting and management trends in each period is significant in providing the basis for proof of this thesis.

Literature Before 1900

A review of management literature before 1900 shows the emergence of scientific management as a solution to the wage problem of labor. This trend is well documented in the Transactions of the American Society of Mechanical Engineers.[13] One of the goals of this society was to consider management problems as part of the mechanical engineer's duties in a business. Immediately, the most frequent problem that was considered by the American Society of Mechanical Engineers was that of wages. Taylor's first article in response to the wage problem, "A Piece Rate System," became the basis of scientific management.

---

[13]For example, see:

F.A. Halsey, "The Premium Plan of Paying for Labor," Trans. ASME, Vol. XII (1891), pp. 755-80.

Henry Towne, "Gain Sharing," Trans. ASME, Vol. X (1889), pp. 600-26.

F.W. Taylor, "A Piece Rate System," Trans. ASME, Vol. XVI (1895), pp. 856-903.

The cost accounting literature before 1900 was generally very sparse. In most cases, there was no demand for anything more than a determination of actual costs. Many companies during this time produced only one product and found little need for sophisticated accounting methods. In addition, cost accounting techniques were considered industrial secrets. Therefore, it was difficult to standardize and popularize accounting techniques.[14] The most notable work during this period was The Cost of Manufactures, by Henry Metcalfe.[15] He attempted to provide the "most probable cost of manufacture"[16] through the extensive use of tickets within the factory. Accounting, as a profession, was not seen as important during this period. Businesses did not see the necessity of having an accountant working in the company. The mechanical engineer took his place in helping to determine the allocation of overhead costs, which was of major concern in this time period.

---

[14] Michael Chatfield, "Accounting Problems of the Industrial Corporation," unpublished manuscript, U.C.L.A. School of Business Administration, Los Angeles, California, 1971, p. 31.

[15] Henry Metcalfe, The Cost of Manufactures and the Administration of Workshops Public and Private (New York: Wiley, 1885).

[16] Henry Metcalfe, "The Shop Order System of Accounts," Trans. ASME, Vol. VII (1886), p. 442.

Literature and Case Studies: 1900-1910

The second chronological period (1900-1910) was chosen since it was a time when scientific management techniques were developing a high level of sophistication. It is during this period that Taylor read his paper, "Shop Management"[17] before the American Society of Mechanical Engineers. In this important paper, he expanded and described his system in sufficient detail to provide for ease of implementation in business. The most important feature of the system was the concept of standards--standardization of tools, shop equipment, supplies, etc. This was a period when scientific management techniques were in use at Bethlehem Iron Company, Yale and Towne Manufacturing, Link Belt Company, Tabor Manufacturing Company, and others. This was a period when Taylor was continuing to develop his system but scientific management had not yet received wide publicity. Perhaps the most important reason for choosing 1910 as an ending point of an era is the great effect that the Eastern Rate Case had on the popularization of both scientific management and standard cost accounting.

In the field of accounting, there was an outburst of literature on cost systems during this period of 1900-1910. A few authors did begin discussing the necessity of "estimates"

---

[17]F.W. Taylor, "Shop Management," Trans. ASME, Vol. XXIV (June, 1903).

and standard cost systems. ". . . as competition grew keener it became necessary to know how much the manufacture of goods was costing and to know as soon as possible after the material was made, and in many cases to figure in advance the probable cost, which required making an estimate."[18] It is also in this period that H.L. Arnold, Alexander H. Church, Harrington Emerson and others began making great contributions to the concept of efficiency in business.

Literature and Case Studies: 1910-1920

The 1910-1920 period saw the full maturation of scientific management techniques and the development of a complete standard cost system. Taylor's system was installed at Acme Hardware, Eastern Manufacturing, Pullman Company and many others. The Society to Promote the Science of Management was begun in 1911 by members of the American Society of Mechanical Engineers "who found it increasingly difficult to get any papers on the subject of management through the Meetings Committee."[19] This was also the time that both Principles of Scientific Management and Shop Management were published which spread the knowledge of scientific

---

[18] Leslie Unckless, How to Find Manufacturing Costs and Selling Costs (Detroit: Modern Methods Publishing Company, 1909), p. 1.

[19] Frank B. Copley, Frederick W. Taylor: Father of Scientific Management (New York: Harper and Brothers, 1923), Vol. II, p. 383. After Taylor's death in 1915, the name of the organization was changed to the Taylor Society.

management far wider than it had known before.[20] In the accounting field, G. Charter Harrison, J. Lee Nicholson, Frank Webner and others developed complete standard cost systems. Finally, for the first time, an abundance of cost accounting literature began being published.

The Historical Setting: 1890-1920

As suggested earlier and as Haber's study suggests, it is important to understand the scientific management movement in the setting of the time. It is only in this way that a full understanding of the development of the standard cost system can be understood. Since these developments have inputs from social, political, and economic events in society, some discussion of the environment in the United States during this period is essential. Further, it can be seen that some of the occurrences during the Progressive era had substantial impact on Frederick Taylor and, thus, on scientific management and standard costing. Therefore, this section will discuss the social, political, and economic environment in the United States between 1890-1920.

The Progressive era, 1890-1920, was a dynamic era in the United States, producing many changes in the social, political and economic composition of the country.

---

[20]Both works were published in 1911 by Harper and Brothers, New York.

> The progressive era is almost made to order for the study of Americans in love with efficiency. For the progressive era gave rise to an efficiency craze--a secular Great Awakening, an outpouring of ideas and emotions in which a gospel of efficiency was preached without embarrassment to businessmen, workers, doctors, housewives, and teachers, and yes preached even to preachers.[21]

The rise of a social awareness or social conscience about the "human condition" has been associated with the writings of the muckrakers. It has been said that the "fundamental critical achievement of American Progressivism was the business of exposure, and journalism was the chief occupational source of its creative writers."[22] The fact that this exposure was a national phenomenon is also important, because of the large numbers of people who for the first time realized the conditions of various segments of their society. It is this era that one finds Upton Sinclair exposing the Chicago meat paking industry and Ida M. Tarbell exposing the Standard Oil Trust. It is in this period that one finds Ray Stannard Baker explaining the collusion among labor unions, and David Graham Phillips blasting the United States Senate as being composed of men who serve interests hostile to the people.

The most socially minded of the muckrakers was Lincoln Steffens. In _Shame of the Cities_, he laid the blame for the

---

[21]Samuel Haber, _Efficiency and Uplift: Scientific Management in the Progressive Era 1890-1920_ (Chicago: University of Chicago Press, 1964), p. ix.

[22]Richard Hofstadter, _The Age of Reform: From Bryan to F.D.R._ (New York: Knopf, 1955), p. 185.

sorrowful human condition on the people and not the government. He called for a sense of responsibility to one's country and to one's fellowman. To this end, he suggested that man should rise up and help those who are in need. He hoped "that our shamelessness is superficial, that beneath it lies a pride which, being real, may save us yet."[23]

Many people responded to Steffens' call. Among them were Jane Addams, Jacob Riis and the large numbers of people who founded the settlement and poor houses around the United States. Poor houses were publicly-run institutions providing a bed and meals for the people who came. Jane Addams relates a sense of idleness, desparity, and degradation felt in these poor houses. In one of Chicago's "County Infirmaries," Jane Addams addresses herself to the lack of motivation among these poor. "To take away from an old woman whose life has been spent in household cares all the foolish little belongings to which her affections cling and to which her fingers have become accustomed is to take away her last incentive to activity, almost to life itself."[24]

Hull House was established by Jane Addams as a settlement house for the urban poor of Chicago. When first established, it

---

[23]Lincoln Steffens, <u>The Shame of the Cities</u> (New York: McClure, Phillips, and Company, 1904), p. 24.

[24]Jane Addams, "Twenty Years at Hull House," in Carl Resek, ed., <u>The Progressives</u> (New York: Bobbs-Merrill Company, Inc., 1967), p. 67.

provided "a day nursery, kindergarten, an employment bureau, and a discussion club."[25] Besides the immediate aid that they provided, they also provided the knowledge of where people could go for both charity and other assistance. All this was done privately, since public welfare was not begun until the New Deal.

We find many women, and generally upper class people in the settlement house movement. For educated women, with career orientations, this kind of work was considered proper and was one of the only professional fields open to them.

There are two theories about upper class involvement in the settlement houses and other reform work. The peer group pressure of the churches was such that one was not considered righteous and wholesome unless he got involved in "saving the sinners" by doing charity work. For the churches, this was the era of social christianity, in which helping one's brother was expected. Secondly, charity, welfare, and aid can be considered forms of social control. The upper class, by aiding the indigent could always keep them in a position of dependency with no threat of upward mobility.

Hofstadter argues that this social conscience and the entire Reform movement is a middle class phenomenon. More recent historical studies indicate that this movement was largely upper class; limited

---

[25] *Ibid.*, p. 65.

to the social elite.[26] In studying the reform movement in Baltimore, James B. Crooks prepared a list of the most active of the reformers, on the basis of newspaper reports of the time. He characterized the group of 108 as generally being upper class, social register, Old Stock American, protestant, well-educated, professional, and young with an average age of 39.

Crooks concluded that among the most important reasons for the reform activity were college education and early childhood experiences. Particularly in Baltimore, at Johns Hopkins University, students were experiencing a new form of education. The school began emphasizing the liberal arts, a relatively new innovation for the time. Previously, universities primarily taught the classics and the hard sciences.[27]

This period also saw the culmination of a tremendous mass migration from Europe to the United States. The flow started in the 1840's with the German and Irish fleeing from the potato famine, and continued in the 1880's with mass migration from Eastern Europe. Regardless of their reasons for leaving--political, economic, or religious--they sought the United States as the land of golden opportunity.

---

[26]See Samuel P. Hays, "The Politics of Reform in Municipal Government in the Progressive Era," Pacific Northwest Quarterly, October, 1964, pp. 157-69.

[27]James G. Crooks, Politics and Progress: The Rise of Urban Progressivism in Baltimore, 1895-1911 (Baton Rouge: LSU Press, 1968).

> Between the close of the Civil War and the outbreak of the first World War, the rise of American Industry and the absence of restrictions drew a steady stream of immigrants, which reached its peak in 1907 when 1,285,000 immigrant entries were recorded. By 1910, 13,345,000 foreign-born persons were living in the United States, or almost one-seventh of the total population.[28]

The immigrants as a whole had considerable impact on society. This was the period immediately after the Industrialization era of 1870 and onward. There was a continuous demand for more workers as new factories were started. Yet, at this time there always seemed to be a surplus of labor. It has been said that

> immigration was good for the rich, the employing class, and a matter of indifference to the short-sighted professional classes with whom immigrants could not compete, but was disastrous for native American workers. Immigrants were strikebreakers, who lowered wage levels and reduced living standards.[29]

Many of the immigrants who landed in the United States were penniless. Many found jobs in factories for long hours and low wages. Still others, because of the labor surplus and discrimination,[30] could not get jobs and were forced to turn to whatever charity they could obtain. Since there was no governmental welfare system at the time, much of the charity was from the political machine.

---

[28]Hofstadter, Age of Reform, p. 176.

[29]Ibid., p. 178.

[30]In New Orleans, Irish were discriminantly excluded from jobs because of their "rowdiness." See Earl F. Niehaus, The Irish in New Orleans, 1800-1860 (Baton Rouge: LSU Press, 1965).

In addition, political machines had the information about other charities and would aid the poor immigrant in whatever way possible. The machine was also able to give out patronage jobs to some of these poor, and would almost certainly provide a turkey for Christmas dinner in return for political support.

Politically, the machines found the base of their support in the low income working class and immigrant population. The machines are often noted for their corruption,[31] but seldom for the functions they performed. The function of the machine and/or its boss was to centralize the power in the community. Thus, the boss system functioned as the friend, helper, and provider of low income people.

Politically, the twentieth century saw the beginnings of reform parties in the major cities attempting to overthrow the "machines." In every major city except Chicago, we see the replacement of the machine with the "good government" parties. Many of these new ideas about city government stem from the philosophies of Richard S. Childs, considered the founding father of the city manager type of government. He believed that there should be nonpartison elections, a short ballot, and a dichotomy between policy and administration.[32] In a book based on interviews

---

[31]Such as Tammany Hall and its notorious leaders: Boss Tweed, Fernando Wood, and George Washington Plunkitt.

[32]See John P. East, Council Manager Government: The Political Thought of Its Founder (Chapel Hill: University of North Carolina Press, 1965).

with Childs, John East claims that the basis for his "ideal" form of government stems from his philosophical background: pragmatism, progressivism, exposure to Tammany Hall, and scientific management. Childs' concept of "the one best way" is directly related to scientific management. In addition, Childs' model is based on a business model that seeks the "most efficient way." The city manager is equated with the chief executive of the corporation, and the councilmen are equated with the board of directors.

Nationally, the political environment of this period is exemplified by the rise of the Progressive Party. The Progressive Party was formed after the Republican National Convention of 1912 renominated President Taft as its candidate. Theodore Roosevelt's determinism to bolt the Republican Party and his dislike for Taft made him a natural leader for the new party.

The Democratic convention, influenced by Theodore Roosevelt's determinism, chose Woodrow Wilson as its candidate. Wilson had previously earned a reputation of being a reformer while president of Princeton University and governor of New Jersey.[33]

The platform of the Progressive Party called for a more direct role of the people in government--direct primaries, direct election of United States Senators, the right of citizens to initiative, referendum, and recall. The platform saw the role

---

[33]Oscar Handlin, The History of the United States (New York: Holt, Rinehart and Winston, 1968), Vol. II, pp. 292-302.

of government as the promotion of the general welfare--woman's suffrage, occupational safety and health standards, minimum wage standards, social insurance for the elderly and disabled, and child labor legislation.

Although Roosevelt's party did not win the election of 1912, it had a decided influence on future governmental policy. "The election of 1912 was ultimately significant for its confirmation of progressive primacy and for its definition of what progressivism meant."[34]

The predominance of the "New Economics" as opposed to the laissez faire concept of Adam Smith began to have its awakening in 1885 with the founding of the American Economic Association. The New Economics clearly showed greater concern for the individual. The platform of the American Economic Association states:

> We regard the state as an educational and ethical agency whose positive aid is an indispensable condition of human progress. While we recognize the necessity of individual initiative in industrial life, we hold that the doctrine of laissez faire is unsafe in politics and unsound in morals; and that it suggests an inadequate explanation of the relations between the state and the citizens.[35]

One of the founders of the A.E.A. and a leading economist of the new school was Richard T. Ely. A leading social reformer of

---

[34] Ibid., p. 302.

[35] From Richard T. Ely, Ground Under Our Feet (New York: The Macmillan Company, 1938), in Carl Resek, ed., The Progressives (New York: The Bobbs-Merrill Company, Inc., 1967), p. 24.

his time, he attacked the theory of individualism--that all men must seek the most wealth for themselves alone. He advocated applying the Christian principle, "all men are brothers," to economics and contended that one day the time will come when

> no decent man will any longer advocate the legitimacy of the universal ways of sharp practice and hard bargaining. Men will then try to put all business relations upon a brotherly basis, and will always inquire what forms of industrial organization and what modes of doing business are in accordance with the highest standards of right, and best promote the general welfare.[36]

Beyond these developments, business experienced tremendous growth amidst economic and political restraints. The Interstate Commerce Act of 1887 and the Sherman Act in 1890 guarded against cheap transportation rates and monopolies.

> General business prosperity, rising prices and an active securities market spurred on this burst of trust formation. Of the 318 trusts listed by Moody in 1904, 82, with a total capitalization of $1,196,700,000, had been organized before 1898. But 234, with a capitalization of over $6,000,000,000 had been organized in the years between January 1, 1898, and January 1, 1904. Thus in this short period almost three-quarters of the trusts and almost six-sevenths of the capital in trusts had come into existence.[37]

This was a period of development of big business. Some of the large companies incorporated during the early 1900's were United States Steel, Standard Oil, Bethlehem Steel, Amalgamated Copper and American Smelting and Refining.

---

[36]Richard T. Ely, Studies in the Evolution of Industrial Society (New York: The Macmillan Press, 1903), p. 430.

[37]Hofstadter, Age of Reform, p. 169.

The Progressive era was a period of rapid change in the political, economic, and social structures in the United States. It is within this period of rapid change that the scientific management movement began due, in part, to the efforts of Frederick W. Taylor. This change caused effects on all aspects of U.S. enterprise and can be seen to have had an important effect on the life of Frederick Taylor. It was during this period that the scientific management movement began and reached its pinnacle of success. Thus, it seems important to understand the political, social, and economic environment under which scientific management and the standard cost system developed. It is with this in mind that the preceding discussion was made.

With an understanding of the historical setting, it is now proper to proceed with a discussion of the history of scientific management and standard cost accounting. Chapter III will discuss the development of cost accounting in the period of 1875-1900 and Chapter IV will discuss the development and importance of scientific management. It is in Chapters V and VI that we will see the interaction of scientific management and the standard cost system.

CHAPTER III

COST ACCOUNTING 1875-1900

Status of Cost Accounting: 1875

The status of cost accounting in 1875 was that of an unsophisticated art. Although the methods of industrial production were being modernized rapidly, there was little demand for more accurate methods of determining costs.

> By the mid-nineteenth century almost no firms were able to show a product's cost flowing from one account to another in the general ledger. Few distinguished between factory overhead and commercial expenses. The techniques for allocating overhead were not generally understood.[1]

Littleton explains that since the development of "factory management" was relatively recent, it is also reasonable that "costing was new."[2] He implies the widely-held belief that costing emanated from a need of management. Littleton continues by stating that:

> Cost accounting appeared in response to needs growing out of the industrialization of business. It undertook to place such detailed information regarding labor and material cost

---

[1]Michael Chatfield, "Accounting Problems of the Industrial Corporation," unpublished manuscript (Los Angeles: University of California, 1971), p. 31.

[2]A.C. Littleton, Accounting Evolution to 1900 (New York: American Institute Publishing Company, 1933), p. 358.

> in the hands of the manager as would enable him to compare his production costs with outside prices for similar work or to estimate on the basis of past records at what price he could afford to contract in undertaking specific production.[3]

Littleton clearly, though, attributes standard costs to "recent accounting contributions to the solution of modern business problems;"[4] the twentieth century.

The philosophical question of whether history arises as a response to an event, need, issue, etc., cannot be resolved easily; for there is no one answer. It does appear, though, that Littleton's point is an important one. If the new factory or production systems had not developed, it is questionable whether cost accounting would have developed at that time. Clearly there was a need for more accurate cost systems and management was demanding those systems so it could make more effective management decisions.

But,

> it was difficult to disseminate knowledge about factory accounting. Cost accounting techniques were considered industrial secrets. Bookkeeping was still dominated by mercentile trading, few texts discussed manufacturing accounting, and few accountants took a generalized view of the subject. Most 'works accountants' did not write down their ideas or methods, and often these were transmitted only when an employee changed jobs.[5]

---

[3] Ibid., pp. 359-60.

[4] Ibid., p. 361.

[5] Chatfield, "Accounting Problems," p. 32.

Cost accounting in 1875 had not reached the same state of evolution that management had. But by the beginning of the twentieth century, management practices became more sophisticated and the need for better cost information was seen. Two separate lag times can be seen. First, the literature gives some evidence that cost accounting practices responded to management's needs, which produced a time lag between new developments in management and new developments in cost accounting. A second time lag existed between the publishing of articles on cost accounting and the adoption of new practices of cost accounting in corporations.[6]

> The last three decades of the nineteenth century were marked by what can only be described as a costing renaissance in the English-speaking world. In the 1880's and 1890's a growing number of writers on costing explained 'new' ideas.[7]

It has been suggested previously that the American Society of Mechanical Engineers took the lead in the advancement of new methods of management, including scientific management. From a thorough review of the accounting literature of this period, it appears that many of the innovative ideas about cost accounting were also presented to the American Society of Mechanical Engineers and also reprinted in the proceedings of their meetings. The papers presented at the meetings as well as the ensuing discussions

---

[6]David Solomons, "The Historical Development of Costing," in David Solomons, ed., Studies in Cost Analysis (Homewood, Ill." Richard D. Irwin, Inc., 1968), pp. 3-50.

[7]*Ibid.*, p. 17.

are most important in attempting to understand the development of cost accounting during this period. This is the primary organization to which cost accounting papers were presented. Further, the proceedings indicate the limited use of cost accounting methods during this period. This is partly because there was little exchange of information about manufacturing and management methods during this period.

During this period (1875-1900), the typical costing system, where such a system existed at all, in manufacturing operations relied on the foreman to provide the information as to the number of labor hours and amount of materials used on each job.

> A check on total wages was kept by the use of a time book kept at the works gate by a timekeeper to record employee's arrival and departure times. . . . Overheads would be added to prime costs of each job usually by adding a flat percentage to labour cost or to prime cost. This percentage would be ascertained from the previous year's financial accounts by expressing the total overhead expenses for the year as a percentage of the year's total direct wages or the total prime costs. The total of these three amounts--direct wages, direct materials and overheads--gave a figure which was accepted as the 'actual' cost of the job.[8]

Most of the writers of this period were able to develop reasonably efficient methods of ascertaining materials and wage costs. Some used card systems; others used elaborate ledger accounts. but, they all resulted in satisfactory ascertainment of prime costs. But, the determination and allocation of overhead expenses caused considerable problems.

---

[8]Ibid., pp. 19-20.

An English Contribution

Although this study is concerned primarily with the effects of scientific management on the development of the standard cost system in the United States, the contribution of Emile Garcke and J.M. Fells in England is of major importance. Their contribution to cost accounting before 1900 stands out as the most important of its kind and essential to the full understanding of the status of cost accounting at this time. Garcke and Fells were the most reputable English cost authorities before 1900.

> Both of these men were important industrial executives and accountants. Garcke held the position of managing director of British Electric Traction Company, and Fells was general manager of Salt Union Limited.[9]

In 1887, Garcke and Fells published their book on factory accounts;[10] it made an important distinction between indirect expense of the factory and other establishment expenses. They found it unacceptable merely to consider direct expenditures in wages and materials to constitute the cost. Rather, they called for:

> distributing all the indirect expenses, such as wages of foremen, rent of factory, fuel, lighting, heating, and cleaning, etc. (but not the salaries of clerks, office rent, stationery and other establishment charges to be referred to later), over the various departments or shops

---

[9]Garner, Cost Accounting to 1925, p. 93.

[10]Emile Garcke and J.M. Fells, Factory Accounts, Their Principles and Practice (London: Crosby, Lockwood and Son, 1887).

> specifically, and in turn distributing the departmental or shop totals over the various working and other orders as a percentage, either upon the wages expended upon the jobs respectively, or upon the cost of both wages and materials.[11]

They felt that the "establishment charges" of office expenses and interest should not be included in the cost of production.

> The establishment charges are, in the aggregate, more or less constant, while the manufacturing costs fluctuate with the cost of labour and the price of material. To distribute the charges over the articles manufactured would, therefore, have the effect of disproportionately reducing the cost of production with every increase, and the reverse with every diminution of business.[12]

Depreciation of machinery was dealt with as a separate problem. They proposed that it could either be included with the indirect expenses of the factory, or by charging each machine:

> with its direct cost of running and maintenance, as well as with its proportion of factory general charges, such as lighting, heating, and power. The charges so made to the Plant or Machinery Ledger would correspondingly reduce the amount of factory general charges, to be otherwise dealt with, and would permit of a more detailed analysis of cost.[13]

Commenting on Garcke and Fells' writing, Brummet stated that:

> Garcke and Fells' position seems now to be far in advance of the times. This is borne out in part by the lack of an immediate general following by their contemporaries. Most of the authorities of these two decades agreed that the

---

[11] _Ibid_., pp. 79-80.

[12] _Ibid_., p. 83.

[13] _Ibid_., p. 81.

> factors which contributed to what is now known as production overhead are different from those causing selling and administration costs and that, therefore, there was some advantage to a segregation of those two groups of overhead costs.[14]

Garcke and Fells illustrate the considerations in costing deemed most important in the period before 1900. As was true with American accountants, Garcke and Fells' attention was focused primarily on the attempt to calculate the actual cost of production. Of major concern was the composition of overhead and the application and allocation of this factory burden. Attention had yet to be drawn to the concepts underlying cost control or to the concept of standard costs. Even where significant advances were made, the managers, the engineers, and the accountants were generally either ignorant or skeptical of these new advances. The journal articles and paper presentations were often looked at with great doubt and contributions often went unnoticed.

Early Examples of Standard Costs

A notable example of one of the more important contributions to the concept of standard costs (as defined on page 7) was that of H.M. Lane. In 1896, he wrote a paper on the determination of factory costs and minimum selling prices. Lane had conducted a study where he

---

[14]R. Lee Brummet, Overhead Costing: The Costing of Manufactured Products (Ann Arbor, Michigan: Bureau of Business Research, School of Business Administration, Univ. of Michigan, 1957), p. 2.

had requested information from about forty firms on the methods followed in cost-keeping in their firm. Some of the responses support the previous claims that businesses were hesitant about telling other firms about their methods. "The question upon which information was sought might be considered delicate and rather an intrusion into matters which might properly be considered confidential."[15] In addition, one firm felt that requests for engineering information would be proper but the problem of attaining better methods for the determination of factory costs and minimum selling prices was "a commercial and not an engineering question."[16]

Lane's study determined that a positive correlation existed between (a) the size and relative prosperity of the firms and (b) the concern for determining better cost-keeping methods. The larger and more prosperous firms were also more willing to provide complete answers to Lane's questions. Lane's study showed that manufacturers, especially small ones, paid little attention to the calculation of minimum selling prices. The smaller firms relied on the larger firms to determine selling prices and thus felt little need for cost calculations.

Lane concluded his paper by making a plea to the American Society of Mechanical Engineers to stop the secretive practices

---

[15]H.M. Lane, "A Method of Shop Accounting to Determine Shop Cost and Minimum Selling Price," Trans. ASME, Vol. XVIII (1896-7), p. 893.

[16]Ibid., p. 892.

prevailing in the industry. He believed that the secrecy was detrimental to the advancement of the art of cost-keeping and that fuller discussion would be mutually beneficial. Only through this full disclosure of cost-keeping and cost control methods could management advance.

Lane heeded his own advice by presenting a paper that proved to be one of the most important contributions of the time. In "A Method of Determining Selling Price," Lane used his engineering background to attempt to apply the engineering concept of standards to modern business management. He proposed a method "by which the conditions affecting the final result of a year's business may be shown in a simple manner at the end of each month or week."[17] This method was to be used as "an auxiliary for the convenience of the manager relating to organization and operation."[18]

An integral part of Lane's approach included a cost sheet comparing actual receipts and expenditures with estimates of those receipts and expenditures.

> This sheet provides for bringing the actual receipts and expenditures together with the estimated, item by item, month by month, so that a glance will show if any item of

---

[17]H.M. Lane, "A Method of Determining Selling Price," Trans. ASME, Vol. XVIII (December, 1896), p. 221.

[18]Ibid., p. 221.

expenditure is actually overrunning the estimated, and if any item of receipts is underrunning the estimated, and show it in time for correction.[19] (See Exhibit I)

Lane's concept of comparing predetermined cost estimates to actual expenses for "correction" is the essence of the standard cost system, variance analysis and management by exception. This appears to be the first instance of a published account of the use of standards in accounting and business management in America. Lane was clearly years ahead of his time. At the time of his writing, business did not see the need to develop standards for costing and did not see the value in his proposals. In the discussion following Lane's papers, comments focused primarily on the determination of actual costs in shops rather than on the usefulness of cost estimates as proposed by Lane.[20]

One obvious drawback of Lane's presentation is that methods for determining the cost estimates were not developed. This drawback could have been one reason that management did not embrace his concept. Businessman may have recognized the need for accurate methods for the setting of standards as contrasted with Lane's reliance on "experience and judgment."[21] Lane was apparently the

---

[19] *Ibid.*, p. 224.

[20] See for example, "A Method of Shop Accounting to Determine Shop Cost and Minimum Selling Price," *Trans. ASME*, Vol. XVIII (1897), pp. 892-900.

[21] Lane, "A Method of Determining Selling Price," pp. 221-27.

EXHIBIT 1

TRANSACTIONS AMERICAN SOCIETY OF MECHANICAL ENGINEERS. VOL. XVIII.

TABLE II., SHEET II.

Expenditures read down.

Month Ending		Jan. 31.	Feb. 28.	Mch. 31.	April 30.	May 31.	June 30.	July 31.	Aug. 31.	Sept. 30.
Profit	Estimated	833.33	1,666.67	2,500.00	3,333.33	4,166.67	5,000.00	5,833.33	6,666.67	7,500.00
	Actual	833.33	1,666.67	2,500.00	3,333.33	4,166.67	5,000.00			
Losses	Estimated	41.66	83.33	125.00	166.66	208.33	250.00	291.66	333.33	375.00
	Actual	....	....	....	100	100	100			
Renewals	Estimated	166.66	333.33	500.00	666.66	833.33	1,000.00	1,166.66	1,333.33	1,500.00
	Actual	50.60	175.30	450.90	730.60	850.43	1,033.70			
Depreciation	Estimated	166.66	333.33	500.00	666.66	833.33	1,000.00	1,166.66	1,333.33	1,500.00
	Actual	166.66	333.33	500.00	666.66	833.33	1,000.00			
Producers' Wages	Estimated	2,083.33	4,166.67	6,250.00	8,333.33	10,416.67	12,500.00	14,583.23	16,666.67	18,750.00
	Actual	2,137.68	4,687.50	6,448.90	8,431.57	11,032.21	13,117.60			
Non.-Pro. Wages	Estimated	2,083.33	4,166.67	6,250.00	8,333.33	10,416.67	12,500.00	14,583.23	16,666.67	18,750.00
	Actual	2,075.61	4,212.13	6,323.00	8,357.91	10,961.13	12,968.90			
Material & Mdse.	Estimated	6,250.00	12,500.00	18,750.00	25,000.00	31,250.00	37,500.00	43,750.00	50,000.00	56,250.00
	Actual	6,111.98	11,361.91	17,321.20	23,911.33	30,671.80	36,139.10			
General Expense	Estimated	833.33	1,666.67	2,500.00	3,333.33	4,166.67	5,000.00	5,833.33	6,666.67	7,500.00
	Actual	891.78	1,741.30	2,684.20	3,486.20	4,364.90	5,236.20			
Stable and Hauling	Estimated	41.66	83.33	125.00	166.66	208.33	250.00	291.66	333.33	375.00
	Actual	42.30	85.40	123.30	160.84	202.90	231.92			
Printing and Stationery	Estimated	25.00	50.00	75.00	100.00	125.00	150.00	175.00	200.00	225.00
	Actual	23.90	51.90	75.60	96.30	131.60	148.40			
Freight and Express	Estimated	41.66	83.33	125.00	166.66	208.33	250.00	291.66	333.33	875.00
	Actual	49.83	96.49	138.60	155.91	201.90	241.60			
Advertising	Estimated	83.33	166.67	250.00	333.33	416.67	500.00	583.83	666.67	750.00
	Actual	83.33	166.67	250.00	333.33	416.67	500.00			
Postage	Estimated	16.67	33.34	50.00	66.67	83.34	100.00	116.67	133.33	150.00
	Actual	17.48	38.70	50.68	61.97	81.38	96.40			
Insurance	Estimated	83.33	166.67	250.00	333.33	416.67	500.00	583.33	666.67	750.00
	Actual	83.33	166.67	250.00	333.33	416.67	500.00			
Commissions	Estimated	16.67	33.34	50.00	66.67	83.34	100.00	167.67	133.33	150.00
	Actual	17.69	33.39	41.60	79.40	96.80	125.60			
Interest and Discounts	Estimated	66.67	133.34	200.00	266.67	333.34	400.00	466.67	533.34	600.00
	Actual	78.30	174.60	278.30	291.20	397.21	483.29			
Charity	Estimated	16.67	33.34	50.00	66.67	83.34	100.00	116.66	133.34	150.00
	Actual	16.67	33.34	50.00	66.67	83.34	100.00			
Legal	Estimated	25.00	50.00	75.00	100.00	125.00	150.00	175.00	200.00	225.00
	Actual	25.00	50.00	75.00	101.25	131.25	260.90			
Fuel	Estimated	41.66	83.33	125.00	166.66	208.33	250.00	291.66	333.33	375.00
	Actual	61.40	98.60	143.80	187.94	210.93	252.40			
Contingent	Estimated	83.33	166.67	250.00	333.33	416.67	500.00	583.33	666.67	750.00
	Actual	....	....	....	340.00	341.67	487.91			
Total Expenditure	Estimated	13,000.00	26,000.00	39,000.00	52,000.00	65,000.00	78,000.00	91,000.00	104,000.00	117,000.00
	Actual	12,766.87	23,623.60	37,701.08	51,229.54	65,692.79	78,373.83			

only writer during this period (1875-1900) who proposed the use of standards in costing and understood conceptually how they were to be used. The focus of other writers of this time period was on accurate cost keeping. Thus, though a complete systematic approach to standard costs was not accomplished, and though Lane's concept was not widely accepted, some advance was made by Lane's contribution to what became standard costing. But, surprisingly, Lane's approach of comparing actual and estimated expenditures has been overlooked by previous accounting historians.

As mentioned earlier, the discussions following papers presented to the American Society of Mechanical Engineers provide important insight into the prevailing views of the period. The discussion following a paper by H.M. Norris[22] provides insight into an important controversy of the time. The argument centered around the question of whether an accurate cost accounting system is a possibility. In his paper, Norris stated: "A cost keeping system to be of real value must forever eliminate all guesswork, and be so designed that it will give accurate results under all conditions of business."[23] In the discussion that followed, Frederick Halsey replied to the "need" for accurate cost accounting methods. He stated that:

---

[22]H.M. Norris, "An Accurate Cost Keeping System," Trans. ASME, Vol. XIX (1898), pp. 387-414.

[23]Ibid., p. 387.

> every manufacturer makes his goods as cheaply as he can, or as he knows how, and sells them for all he can get, and the question of niceties in cost-keeping does not have much to do with either the income or the outgo of the business. While, therefore, these things are interesting and of importance, I do not think they are of such vast importance as a good many people think.[24]

In reply to the same statement, W.S. Rogers states:

> I do not think we will ever find an accurate cost system that will fit all conditions in all factories. We may take all the literature on cost-keeping in existence and find it will fit here and there about the earth, but not all points of the compass.[25]

In all of the discussions at the end of Norris' paper, the discussants first related their own methods of cost finding in use at their firms, and then either criticized or complimented Norris on his work. One of the discussants, C.W. Hunt, invited other members of the Society to view the system in operation in his company. "There are no secrets, and I invite all to visit us who take an interest in the subject."[26] This statement, as noted earlier, was rare for the time and a step forward in the attempt to exchange information so that better cost systems could be developed.

---

[24] *Ibid.*, p. 400.

[25] *Ibid.*, p. 403.

[26] *Ibid.*, p. 407.

The System of Henry Metcalfe

The most well known works on cost accounting of this period (1875-1900), were those of Captain Henry Metcalfe.[27] The object of his complex system of tickets for every order and every expense is to:

> Provide automatic, and therefore impartial means of determining the most probable cost of manufactures in gross, or in such detail as the expense of its determination may permit . . . . By thus defining every charge for labor and material, our accounts are, so to speak, balanced in advance, and it only remains to distinguish between specific and general expenses and properly to apportion the general expenses among the specific, in order to obtain the most probable cost of any specific object.[28]

Though important and advanced for his time, Metcalfe's concept of the "most probable cost" is not a standard cost. He was attempting here to develop an accurate system of determining actual costs and to centralize this within the management structure.

He defines the cost of doing work as the net cost (labor and material minus direct expenses) plus the gross cost (indirect expenses). In determining the gross cost, he determines a cost factor for each department as follows:

---

[27]Captain Henry Metcalfe, The Cost of Manufactures (New York: John Wiley and Sons, 1885). Also, see his article, "The Shop Order System of Accounts," Trans. ASME, Vol. VII (1886), pp. 440-88.

[28]Metcalfe, "Shop Order System of Accounts," pp. 442-43.

1. To distribute such general expenses as rent, insurance, taxes, etc., among departments profiting by them according to the most probable hypothesis.

2. To distribute last year's general standing orders or the unclassifiable current expenses among departments in proportion to the total day's work done in each department.

3. To add this amount for each department to the sum of its own expenses for the past year, as given by the cost of its departmental order.

4. To divide the gross amount thus obtained by the number of direct days' work done in each department during the past year, and so obtain a cost factor, say of $1.15 per day, by which the cost of every day's direct work in the present year must be increased in order to make it bear its most probable share of the cost of facilities provided for it.[29]

As can be seen from the above quote, Metcalfe made a significant contribution to the attempt to determine actual costs of production. In this paper, he received some notable comments. One, from Taylor, discusses Taylor's experience at the Midvale Steel Company. He states that the system there is very similar to that of Metcalfe's:

> The chief idea in our system, as in his, is that the authority for doing all kinds of work should proceed from one central office to the various departments, and that there proper records should be kept of the work and reports made daily to the central office, so that the superintending department should be kept thoroughly informed as to what is taking place throughout the works, and at the same time no work could be done in the works without proper authority.

---

[29] Ibid., p. 456.

> The details of the system have been very largely modified as time went on, and a consecutive plan, such as Mr. Metcalfe proposed, would have been of great assistance to us in carrying out our system.[30]

Although Metcalfe's work is important in that it clearly shows us the state of the art in 1885, Littleton claims that the book:

> . . . must be regarded as insufficient from an accounting point of view, for the author in the end (p. 289) confesses his inability to present a method for proving the cost sheets by the cash accounts (i.e., of 'tying-in' the cost records and the general records). Another explanation of its inadequacy is the fact that the book is concerned mostly with shop management in a government arsenal where there are no problems of capital or entrepreneur's profit. It describes, therefore, not a system of accounts, but the 'paper work' of army accountability, so arranged as to enable the officers in charge to compare their results with the prices for similar work in the open market. Captain Metcalfe strongly advocates the use of cards for all original records. This practice speeds up recording procedure by permitting varied sortings of data before tabulation and summarization and is, therefore, greatly superior to books for original records. The idea is much in favor in modern systems and, apparently, was here applied to factory records for the first time.[31]

Metcalfe's works are important. In some ways his book may be incomplete. His paper to the American Society of Mechanical Engineers is important, as Taylor points out. It does provide a systematic framework for the calculation of actual costs of production. It may have even pushed the field along by developing this systematic approach. But, the concept of standard costs was not yet developed.

---

[30] Ibid., p. 475.

[31] A.C. Littleton, Accounting Evolution to 1900 (New York: American Institute Publishing Company, 1933), p. 355.

The Emphasis on Cost-Finding

Another prominent author of the period, George L. Fowler, suggests some form or elements of standard cost accounting in his article, "Estimating the Cost of Foundry Work."[32] In commenting on Fowler's work, Garner states: "It is the opinion of the present writer that it (ratio of wages to indirect costs) was to be a predetermined figure."[33] Fowler attempted to arrive at predetermined amounts, but their comparison with actual costs is not well described. He does not indicate explicitly how the "estimates" are to be arrived at. Further, he proposed his estimate not for cost control but rather to estimate the product cost at one point in time so that selling price can be determined. Thus, though he used the concept of predetermined costs, it must be said, in retrospect, that Fowler's methods are not fully developed in comparison with the cost accounting systems resulting from the scientific management era.

The major accounting thrust during this era was towards cost finding.[34] W.G. Nichols, a prominent cost accountant, gives a good example of cost finding in a book published at the turn of

---

[32]George L. Fowler, "Estimating the Cost of Foundry Work," Trans. ASME, Vol. IX (1887), pp. 390-97.

[33]Garner, Cost Accounting to 1925, p. 205.

[34]As defined in Chapter I.

the twentieth century.[35] He proposed his book as a "method for the determination as far as may be practicable of the costs of manufacture in an establishment."[36] He addressed himself to the "departments of cost determination" and his interest in determining all of the actual costs.

Writing during the same era, C.A. Millener defines cost accounts as "the practical records of materials and expenditures through the various stages of the manufacture of enterprise, and the determining at each stage the value of the resulting finished or unfinished product."[37] This definition explains the overwhelming concern of accountants at this time to determine accurate costs. The accounting systems were so inadequate for finding the actual costs of production, that is was an important achievement when they could develop complete systems of cost accounts.[38]

---

[35]W.G. Nichols, Cost Finding in Cotton Mills (Waltham, Mass.: Press of E.L. Barry, 1900).

[36]Ibid., p. 50.

[37]C.A. Millener, "The Evolution of Cost Accounts," Business, July, 1895, p. 266.

[38]Cost accounts, ad defined by Millener, meant the classification of systematized and accurately kept accounts.

Summary

Though there were other articles about cost accounting during the period 1875-1900, the major ones have been discussed.[39] The thrust of cost accounting during this period was towards a better determination of actual costs of production. Any mentions of concepts of predetermined standards were not well developed nor well received. Businessmen had not yet realized the value of having standard costs and had not yet seen a need for such information. With the development of scientific management, it will be argued, management saw a need for this information and pressed for its integration into the overall management framework.

---

[39]Those with deep interest may want to see: Henry Leon Binsee, "A Short Way to Keep Time and Cost," Trans. ASME, Vol. IX (1887), pp. 380-89.

Albert Fink, Cost of Railroad Transportation (Louisville: J.P. Morton & Co., 1875).

A.J. Shaw, "Machine Shop Time and Cost Accounts," American Machinist, 1886, pp. 3-4.

Henry Roland, "Cost Keeping Methods in Machine Shop and Foundry," Engineering Magazine, Vol. XIV (1897-98), pp. 56-63, 225-38, 464-72, and 626-34.

Henry Roland, "An Effective System of Finding and Keeping Shop Costs," Engineering Magazine, Vol. XV (1898), pp. 77-86, 241-50, 395-400, 610-20, 749-58, and 1000-1016.

CHAPTER IV

THE DEVELOPMENT OF SCIENTIFIC MANAGEMENT

Some writers maintain that the history of management thought began in the 1900's with the scientific management movement.[1] But, the setting for the development of scientific management was set in the latter half of the nineteenth century. Thus, it is important to give some explanation of the status of management thought and practice in the period directly preceding the development of scientific management. Scientific management can be seen as a response to the needs of management and society. Its evolution from earlier management developments is thus important.

Status of Management in 1875 as Exemplified by the Railroads

In 1875, the status of management was closely related to the status of the railroads, since the railroads were among the first large corporate enterprises in the United States. Thus, in describing the status of management, something must be said about the railroads--one of the first "business enterprises requiring

---

[1]See for example, Daniel A. Wren, *The Evolution of Management Thought* (New York: The Ronald Press Company, 1972), p. 146.

massive capital investment and calling for complex administrative arrangements."[2] The railroads transformed a generally agrarian economy into an industrial economy directed at production goods. As a means of transportation, the railroads brought the nation closer together. It was now much easier to ship consumer goods from the Eastern Seaboard to the Western states. "The construction of the American railroads was stimulated almost wholly by the demand for better transportation to move crops, to bring farmers supplies, and to open up new territories to commercial agriculture."[3] This brought about the demand for producers goods and ultimately the demand for consumer goods. By 1893, the first large corporations began to develop partly due to the expansion that the railroads encouraged.[4]

Regardless of how much importance is placed on the development of the railroads and their contribution to the second Industrial

---

[2]Alfred D. Chandler, Jr., "The Coming of Big Business," in Alfred D. Chandler, Jr.; Stuart Bruchey; and Louis Galambos, eds., The Changing Economic Order: Readings in American Business and Economic History (New York: Harcourt, Brace and World, Inc., 1968), p. 270.

[3]Alfred D. Chandler, Jr., "The Beginnings of 'Big Business' in American Industry," in James P. Baughman, ed., The History of American Management (Englewood Cliffs, N.J.: Prentice-Hall, Inc., 1969), p. 4.

[4]For example, Swift Company, American Tobacco Company, Singer Sewing Machine Company, and Carnegie Steel. A more extensive discussion of this facet of American business history can be seen in Chandler, Ibid., pp. 1-28.

Revolution in America, it must be acknowledged that the railroads were the first large corporate enterprises in the United States. One of the important innovative changes that occurred due to the rise of big business was the increasing importance of control to organizations. Before the appearance of the railroad companies, most companies were relatively small. As businesses grew in size, their organizational forms became more complex and a need was seen for tighter control. Management attempted to become more systematic and with increased delegation of authority the need for better information for decisions was seen. Experimentation began to determine better ways to manage a large organization and many of these new forms of organization were put into practice in the most innovative of the organizations--the railroads.

The Pennsylvania Railroad Corporation, at the end of its expansion, controlled and operated all lines east of Pittsburgh, Chicago, and St. Louis. "The Pennsylvania complex legal structure became the standard model for the other great railroad systems that emerged in its wake, and it permanently solved the knotty legal problem of how a corporation chartered in one state could safely and effectively extend into other states."[5] Under the leadership of

---

[5]Alfred D. Chandler, Jr., and Stephen Salsbury, "The Railroads: Innovators in Modern Business Administration," in Aldred D. Chandler, et. al., <u>The Changing Economic Order: Readings in American Business and Economic History</u> (New York: Harcourt, Brace and World, Inc., 1968), pp. 249-50.

J. Edgar Thomson[6] the company prospered. "Thomson created a 'decentralized' managerial structure designed to facilitate control at all levels despite the corporation's enormous size."[7] Though the corporation prospered under this decentralized structure and though the other railroads often followed the Pennsylvania's lead in management innovation, the centralized structure came to dominate many of the railroad corporations. The Illinois Central was a good example of a highly centralized structure. The railroad was bought in 1883 by a group of New York financiers who immediately set out to change the railroad's administrative structure. "For advice they relied heavily on the Illinois Central's old operating executives,"[8] who favored a highly centralized structure. The departments reported directly to the officials in the Chicago headquarters. Though there were benefits to the centralized structure,

> The centralized management blurred the distinction between routine operational matters and broad entrepreneurial decisions.

---

[6]J. Edgar Thomson was the president of the Pennsylvania Railroad from 1852 until 1874. He pioneered in the introduction of a line and staff system in 1857, and many of the other railroads followed his example.

[7]Alfred D. Chandler, Jr., and Stephen Salsbury, <u>The Changing Economic Order</u>, p. 250.

[8]<u>Ibid</u>., p. 253.

> In the long run, top executives tended to get so involved in day-to-day problems that they had little time to devote to setting over-all policies and strategies.[9]

The concept of control also entered very heavily into the American manufacturing industries from 1875-1900. "The general line of argument was that as a result of their very success and growth American firms had reached a point at which internal operations had become increasingly chaotic, confused, and wasteful."[10] The attempt of many writers of the time[11] was to attack these problems by suggesting different forms of managerial structure or by simply identifying the severe problems very clearly.

For example, Arnold discusses the breakdown in relationships between top and lower level management.[12] He notes that there was a deterioration of effective control over subordinates by top level

---

[9] Ibid., pp. 253-54.

[10] Joseph A. Litterer, "Systematic Management Design for Organizational Recoupling in American Manufacturing Firms," in James P. Baughman, ed., The History of American Management: Selections from the Business History Review (Englewood Cliffs, N.J.: Prentice-Hall, Inc., 1969), p. 54. Also see, Joseph A. Litterer, "Systematic Management: The Search for Order and Integration," Business History Review, Vol. XXXV (Winter, 1961), pp. 461-76.

[11] Such writers as Alexander H. Church, Henry Metcalfe, H.M. Norris, H.F.L. Orcutt, and Horace Arnold were very prolific in this time period.

[12] Henry Roland (Horace L. Arnold), "An Effective System of Finding and Keeping Shop Costs," Engineering Magazine, Vol. XV (April, 1898), pp. 77-78.

management. Top level management did not receive adequate information about the organizational affairs below them and were thus not able to manage effectively.

At the same time, other writers were developing methods for the reduction of waste and for increased control. One of the first production-control systems to be presented in detail was that used by the Yale Lock Manufacturing Company. Developed by Henry R. Towne, at the time president of the company, it was first publicly described in 1882.[13]

> It operated in the following fashion: Upon receipt of an order from a customer the office would prepare an order, today we would call it a shop order, for the factory. For this a specialized two-part form had been developed. Each order would be identified by its own number. The shop order would then be sent to the production superintendent who would in turn forward it to the department foreman whom he thought should be responsible for the order. Upon receipt of the shop order the foreman would determine the date the order would be completed, put this date on the form, and send half of the form back to the production superintendent.[14]

"The managers of these consolidations (railroads) soon discovered that the administration of the large railroad organizations posed a completely new set of problems from those encountered in

---

13See Henry R. Towne, "Shop Systems of the Yale Lock Manufacturing Company," American Machinist, Vol. V (February 18, 1882).

14Litterer, "Systematic Management," pp. 61-62.

their smaller enterprises."[15] As if to answer these problems, Henry Poor, editor of the American Railroad Journal (1849 to 1862) set out to establish basic managerial principles for large business organizations.

Fundamentally, Poor argues that the railroad managers needed to be guided by only three principles: organization, communication, and information--with organization, or the careful division of work, the most fundamental of all. He proposed that a railroad's organization should be designed to insure that each man's time was fully utilized and the railroad's equipment was kept in service as fully as possible. By communication, Poor envisioned a reporting system which would keep management informed of the operations at all times. The information principle was described as the analyzing of reports to improve operations.[16]

The bridge between management practices in 1875 on the one hand and the rise of the scientific management movement on the other is the increased industrialization[17] that took place in most business enterprises. The shift to industrialization necessitated

---

[15]Claude S. George, Jr., The History of Management Thought (Englewood Cliffs, N.J.: Prentice-Hall, Inc., 1968), p. 78.

[16]Ernest Dale, The Great Organizers (New York: McGraw Hill Book Company, 1960), p. 19.

[17]Industrialization is here defined as that process which transforms the mechanisms of production from manual to mechanical.

greater capital investments by entrepreneurs bringing about increased risks. This further brought about the necessity for increased control of costs. Because one of the underlying principles of scientific management was the control of costs, the concept of production control had its renaissance with the rise in influence of the scientific management movement.

The Origin of Scientific Management

Scientific management, as defined previously, is a system that attempts to increase worker efficiency by setting standards for the worker, the quality of his equipment, and the method of doing work. The basis for achieving these standards is elementary time study, which breaks down each element of work so that a basis may be laid for the development of standards.

Though most management textbooks refer to Frederick W. Taylor as the father of scientific management, evidence shows that he, along with Harrington Emerson, Alexander Church, Frederick Halsey, Frank Gilbreth, Henry Gantt and others, developed the concepts but not the terminology. In the writings of Taylor, the term "scientific management" only appears by accident. He used it occasionally when explaining his ideas to visitors at his home in Chestnut Hill, Philadelphia.[18] Part of the reason for this was that the idea itself was unfamiliar to most people. Fifty years before Taylor's time, Charles Babbage[19] had touched lightly on many of the ideas that were later contained in Taylor's system but the concepts did not spread. Babbage suggests:

> . . . the extension of specialization beyond manual labor to mental labor, which is at the basis of the Taylor doctrines of functional foremanship and the separation of planning from execution. Babbage also fore-shadows the use of timing as an aid in the development of processes; but in this he was not so fortunate, and the undeveloped method he used is not even remotely connected with modern time study.[20]

The Eastern Rate Case

The association of the term "scientific management" with its principles is largely due to the efforts of Louis Brandeis, one of the attorneys opposing proposed railroad rate increases. In 1910, the railroads north of the Ohio and Potomac Rivers and east of the Mississippi applied to the Interstate Commerce

---

[18]Horace B. Drury, Scientific Management: A History and Criticism (New York: Author published, 1915), p. 16. It should be noted that the discussion presented in the remainder of this chapter follows closely that proposed by Drury. This work is well respected as an authority on scientific management.

[19]Charles Babbage, Cost of Manufactures (London, 1832).

[20]Clarence Bertrand Thompson, The Theory and Practice of Scientific Management (Boston: Houghton Mifflin Company, 1917), pp. 176-77.

Commission for substantially higher freight rates. The railroads defended the proposed new rates by claiming increased operating costs due to wage increases.

Brandeis' position during the hearings in September, October and November of 1910 were that operating costs could be substantially decreased by the application of the principles of "scientific management." To prove his point some of the leaders of the movement testified before the Interstate Commerce Commission on November 21.[21] The witnesses testified that in their experience, applying the principles of scientific management had increased the output per workman at least two or three times. One of the witnesses testified "that the railroads of the United States might save $1,000,000 a day by paying greater attention to efficiency of operation."[22] The witnesses had agreed beforehand, in a meeting with Brandeis, to use consistently the term "scientific management" rather than the variety of other names in use at the time.[23]

21"Brandeis Tells How U.S. Railroads Can Save $1,000,000 a Day," Philadelphia North American, November 21, 1910.

22"Roads Could Save $1,000,000 a Day," New York Times, November 22, 1910.

23Such names in use at the time were "Taylor System," "Functional Management," "Shop Management," and "Efficiency."

The introduction of scientific management to the public began with these hearings. By January, 1911, Railway Age Gazette began a series on the implications of scientific management to the railroads.[24] In October, 1911, Dartmouth College held a conference to spread information about scientific management.[25] In 1913, a bibliography was published of the "efficiency" literature written between 1898 and 1913.[26] From this bibliography Drury compiled the following table:

Articles whose titles contain the term "scientific management"[27]

Prior to the rate-advance hearings	None
During December, 1910	2
During 1911	26
During 1912	14

From this bibliography the following list was compiled:

All Periodical Articles on Efficiency Subjects

1907	8	1910 (6 of these in Dec.)	15
1908	5	1911	59
1909	7	1912	38

---

[24]This was one of the leading railroad journals of the time. The series ran from January to July, 1911.

[25]See Addresses and Discussions at the Conference on Scientific Management, October 12, 13, and 14, 1911. First Tuck School Conference, Dartmouth College Conferences. (Published by the Amos Tuck School of Administration and Finance, Hanover, 1911.)

[26]H.H.B. Meyer, "Select List of References on Scientific Management and Efficiency," Efficiency Number of Special Libraries (Washington, D.C.: Library of Congress, 1913).

[27]Drury, Scientific Management, p. 20.

The impact of the Eastern Rate hearings on the popularization of scientific management can be seen to have been very significant. This will be proven to be significant again as the development of the standard cost literature is traced.

The historical development of scientific management is chronicled best in the Transactions of the American Society of Mechanical Engineers. Mechanical engineers first began applying control concepts to business as a solution to the wages problem.

Solution to the Wages Problem

The meetings of the American Society of Mechanical Engineers were where many of the important contributions[28] to the principles of scientific management were made. The Society was organized in 1880, and in 1884 adopted as an objective the promotion of the Arts and Sciences connected with Engineering and Mechanical Construction. The Society later enlarged their function by considering management problems as well. The reasons for this

---

[28]Some of the most important papers were: F.W. Taylor, "Shop Management," Trans. ASME, Vol. XXIV; J.M. Dodge, "A History of the Introduction of A System of Shop Management," Trans. ASME, Vol. XXVII; F.A. Halsey, "The Premium Plan of Paying for Labor," Trans. ASME, Vol. XXII; F.W. Taylor, "A Piece Rate System," Trans. ASME, Vol. XVI; Henry R. Towne, "Gain Sharing," Trans. ASME, 1889, Vol. X; Henry Metcalfe, "The Shop Order System of Accounts," Trans. ASME, Vol. VII. Some of the best contributions to the literature are found in the discussions at the end of papers presented.

are contained in a paper of Henry R. Towne[29] read before the Society in 1886. The substance of the argument was as follows: The final value of the work of a mechanical engineer depends on whether or not the employer makes money out of his business: but the making of money depends not only on seeing that the technical matters connected with manufacture are intelligently looked after. To a surprisingly large extent, work-management and the methods of dealing with employees react on costs. In this lucrative field, who can accomplish more than one strong man charged with the management of the shop as a whole? But the person exercising this authority must be a man of engineering training and practical experience, not a clerk or accountant only. Mr. Towne concludes by proposing that the Society undertake to gather by means of papers presented before its meetings, a stock of information with regard to the little understood art of management.

As the Society began to consider problems of management, the one which received most of their effort was the wages problem. Two basic wage schemes were considered: the day work plan and the piece work plan. It was felt that under the day work plan, men did not work to their fullest capacity. Halsey stated that "matters naturally settle down to an easy going pace, in which

---

[29]Henry R. Towne, "The Engineer as an Economist," Trans. ASME, Vol. VII (1886).

the workmen have little interest in their work, and the employer pays extravagantly for his product."[30] Taylor observed that men were paid for the position they filled, rather than the work they did. He felt that this was demoralizing for the worker and that the worker had no incentive to work hard.

The piece work plan, on the other hand, was based on output. It was hoped that this plan would offset the apparent difficulties in day work as employees had monetary incentives to increase their output. But, as the worker produced more and increased his wage, the employer felt that his payroll was too high and cut the piece rates.

> The cutting of rates has occurred so frequently and invariably in factory life that workmen have learned what to expect. So labor unions frequently limit the earnings of their members--and thus the output.[31]

The first notable attempt at a solution to the wage problem by a member of the American Society of Mechanical Engineers was proposed in a paper by Henry Towne.[32] His plan, a form of profit sharing, attempted to isolate those components of production costs

---

[30]F.A. Halsey, "The Premium Plan of Paying for Labor," Trans. ASME, Vol. XII, p. 755.

[31]Drury, Scientific Management, p. 34.

[32]Henry Towne, "Gain Sharing," Trans. ASME, Vol. X (1889), pp. 600-626. In June, 1887, William Kent presented a paper, "A Problem in Profit Sharing," Trans. ASME, Vol. VIII. This plan, though similar to Towne's, did not include the detailed description that Towne's did.

which the laborer could influence and base the division or sharing of profits upon the amount of reduction in these costs. The plan was drawn up in the form of a contract. The contract prices, which were the original costs, were often fixed at reduced rates by the employer. The employer's justification was that by increased worker effort, a considerable reduction in costs would take place. The gain sharing plan was put into operation in the works of the Yale & Towne Mfg. Co., in January, 1887, and by May, 1889, some 300 workers were employed under the system. The workers had drawn dividends of about four or five per cent of their yearly earnings. The plan was abandoned, though, in the 1890's so that the company could introduce scientific management.

Another important paper on the wage problem was presented by Halsey in 1891.[33] His plan was an adaptation of piece work. He proposed to change the piece work system so that rate cutting would never be necessary.

> His method consists in first determining the time which the men have been taking to do their work, and then announcing that if they will finish it quicker, they will be given, in addition to their old rate, a new premium rate of so much an hour for the time saved. This premium rate is always less than the day rate.[34]

---

[33]Frederick A. Halsey, "The Premium Plan of Paying for Labor," Trans. ASME, Vol. XII (1891), pp. 755-80.

[34]Drury, Scientific Management, p. 43.

The premium plan was first applied by William Kent in the works of the Springer Torsion Balance Company. F.W. Taylor, first in 1895, and again in his classic paper on "Shop Management" (1903), considered Halsey's paper a modification of the Towne gain sharing system. Taylor saw both Towne's plan and Halsey's plan as being related since neither attempted to determine scientifically the exact amount of production that a man is able to produce. This became one of the fundamental principles of Taylor's system.

Before Taylor's writings, the papers generally discussed attempts to increase productivity through different wage plans and other forms of motivation for the worker. Their basic failure was that they did not define the elements of product output or work. They considered the work process to be given, and attempted to change the workers. Taylor's system, on the other hand, was logically more complete. He first changed the process and order of work, and thus, the workers would necessarily have to adapt to these new work processes. This, he felt, would culminate in the highest amount of productivity and the highest wages for workers.

Taylor and Scientific Management

In 1895, Taylor[35] presented, "A Piece Rate System," to

---

[35]Among Taylor's chief writings are the papers read before the American Society of Mechanical Engineers: "A Piece-Rate System," (1895), "Shop Management," (1903), and "On the Art of

the American Society of Mechanical Engineers.[36] This was his first published article on his system of scientific management, although he had installed this system, in part, at the Midvale Steel Company beginning in 1883 with the start of his employment there. Taylor's main objective in developing scientific management was to find a solution to the wage problem.

> Taylor's method of attacking the wages problem consisted in an improvement of piece-work by virtue of which rate cutting was to be eliminated. The originality in Taylor's scheme consisted, however, neither in his view of the problem, nor in his singling out of rate cutting as a target for reform. It was when he offered his scientific proposal as to how rate-cutting might be avoided that the construction of his own unique system began.[37]

Taylor proposed that elementary time studies be performed on each job. This involved the analysis of each elementary movement of both man and machine, that, when combined in proper

---

Cutting Metals," (1906). With S.E. Thompson he wrote Concrete, Plain and Reinforced (1905), and Concrete Costs (1911). His philosophy is, however, best expressed in The Principles of Scientific Management (1911). His system is also explained in periodical articles, in numerous addresses, in testimony before the special House committee which investigated scientific management (1911-12), and in testimony before the Industrial Relations Commission (April, 1913).

[36]Frederick W. Taylor, "A Piece Rate System Being a Step Toward Partial Solution of the Labor Problem," Trans. ASME, Vol. XVI (1895), pp. 856-903. This paper consists primarily of descriptions of methods and results of a system Taylor installed. It is in his later works, such as The Principles of Scientific Management that Taylor discusses his system in a conceptual framework.

[37]Drury, Scientific Management, pp. 54-55.

order, result in the job's being done. A good example of an elementary time study is found in Taylor's writings:

Analysis by Elementary Time Study of the Planing of a Surface on a Piece of Cast Iron[38]

Work Done by Man	Minutes or Seconds
Lift piece from floor to planer table	_______
Level and set work true on table	_______
Put on stops and bolts	_______
Remove stops and bolts	_______
Remove piece to floor	_______
Clean machine	_______
Work Done by Machine	
Rough off cut 1/4 in. thick, 4 ft. long, 2 1/2 in. wide	_______
Rough off cut 1/8 in. thick, 3 ft. long, 12 in. wide, etc.	_______
Finish cut 4 ft. long, 2 1/2 in. wide	_______
Finish cut 3 ft. long, 12 in. wide, etc.	_______
Total	_______
Add _______________ per cent for unavoidable delays	_______

At first glance elementary time study appears to be an expensive and tedious job. In actuality, though, once the initial studies are made, little else must be done. Since all of these elements usually appear over and over again in different jobs, it is merely a matter of determining the elements in a job and adding up the minutes and seconds in order to determine how long

---

[38]F.W. Taylor, "A Piece Rate System," p. 871.

the new job should take. The main reason, though, for the development of elementary time study was to secure accuracy of the results, and be able to use this in a predictive manner. It provided accurate data for fixing:

> piece rates which it will never be necessary to cut. In a word, elementary time study, according to the advocates of scientific management, is the key to the solution of the wages problem.[39]

Differential Rate

Another important concept introduced by Taylor in "A Piece Rate System" is the differential rate. The differential piece rate system paid a low rate per piece for a small output, and a higher rate per piece for a larger output. Its purpose was to encourage the workers to work at the maximum rate which elementary time study had established as possible of achieving. The system adversely affected the worker whose output was low and did not work at the standard rate (as determined by the time study). For those whose output was high, the wage was substantially higher than that under the ordinary piece work plan.

The effect of elementary time study, the differential rate, and a policy of never cutting rates was:

1. The removal of restrictions on output due to the fear of rate cutting.

---

[39]Drury, Scientific Management, p. 59.

2. Production at a maximum due to the differential rate.

3. The maintenance of the set standard by the workmen, since their earnings are sufficiently above the average to make them content.[40]

In testimony before a special committee of the House of Representatives, investigating the Taylor system of shop management, Taylor defended the positive effects of his system on the worker. He presented a statistical chart as evidence of how worker wages had improved since the adoption of the Taylor system at the Tabor Manufacturing Company (Exhibit 2).

> The statement gives the name of the man, the original date of his employment, his first occupation, the price at which he hired himself to that company when he first came, his present occupation, and his average wages earned per hour during the week . . . , and the statement then gives the percentage of increase in the pay which each man has received since he first entered the employ of the company . . . . the men who come under scientific management are taught how to do a better and higher class of work than they did before, and they are given a finer and higher class of work to do with the accompanying higher pay.[41]

"Shop Management"

"Shop Management" is an expansion of the earlier paper, "A Piece Rate System" and includes much of the detailed methods that were developed by Taylor, together with some analysis of the

---

[40] Ibid., p. 62.

[41] Hearings Before Special Committee of the House of Representatives to Investigate The Taylor and Other Systems of Shop Management Under Authority of House Res. 90, Vol. III (January 30, 1912), p. 273.

EXHIBIT 2

STATISTICS OF WAGES OF TABOR MFG. CO.

AT TIME OF EMPLOYMENT				PRESENT DATE		
Name of Employee	Date	Occupation	Rate at which Employed	Occupation	Average Wages Earned	Percent. of Increase
			Per Hour		Per Hour	
Allibone, W.	6/22/05	Tool boy	$0.12	Machinist	$0.31	158
Angerman, C.	6/ 3/04	Machinist	.24	Vise hand	.36	50
Anderson, C.	12/ 3/09	Machinist	.26	Machinist	.39	50
Bradley, G.	10/17/02	Machinist	.25	Machinist	.41	64
Bierchank, W.	9/10/04	Machinist's helper	.15	Machinist	.46	207
Bryson, D.	10/29/06	Colored laborer	.16	Machinist's helper	.23	44
Blackwell, W.	2/16/05	Colored janitor	.18	Janitor	.22	22
Brogan, P.	6/27/07	Drill press	.18	Milling Machine	.31	72
Bruan, S.	10/20/10	Timekeeper	.22	Timekeeper	.24	11
Bardsley, A.	1/ 5/10	Pattern maker	.28	Pattern maker	.38	36
Boasman, W.	3/ 3/10	Colored tool boy	.16	Tool boy	.19	19
Carter, J.	1/12/03	Machinist	.25	Gang foreman	.54	118
Clark, H.	3/12/10	Apprentice, lathe	.16	Turret lathe	.18	13
Cox, C.	1/ 1/1900	Laborer	.15	Machinist	.40	167
Chadwick, B.	1/10/10	Machinist	.28	Machinist	.37	32
Connelly, H.	8/10/03	Blacksmith	.31½	Blacksmith	.47	49
Evans, W.	6/19/05	Machinist	.22½	Machinist	.34	51
Freck, J.	5/31/05	Machinist	.25	Machinist	.40	60
Foreman, E.	3/ 1/05	Machinist	.25	Machinist	.32	28
Field, M.	8/29/06	Colored machinist helper	.18	Laborer	.22	22
Goodwin, C.	8/19/09	Milling, under instruction	.16	Machinist	.34	113
Hamilton, J.	5/26/01	Pipe fitting	.18	Pipe fitting	.26	45

industrial and economic principles involved in his system. In "Shop Management,"[42] Taylor re-emphasizes the importance of securing the initiative of the workmen and of finding the best workmen for the job, since he believed that they could produce substantially more than the average workmen.

In this paper, he further deals with the introduction of efficiency into the operations of the factory. The most clear-cut path to efficiency was through the standardization of tools and equipment. It was found through time studies that machines of the same type but in different condition performed a job in varying times. Thus, the man who worked an inferior machine would ultimately earn less, since it would take longer to complete each job. Taylor was not concerned with having the best equipment, though, but rather that the equipment be "uniform" throughout the factory. This, he felt, was directly connected with worker motivation. Taylor continues:

> But what is, perhaps of more importance still, the rate fixing department has shown the necessity of carefully systematizing all of the small details in the running of each shop; such as the care of belting, the proper shape of cutting tools, and the dressing, grinding and issuing of same, oiling machines, issuing orders for work, obtaining accurate labor and material returns, and a host of other minor methods and processes. These details, which are usually regarded as of comparatively small importance, and many of which are left to the individual judgment of

---

[42] Frederick W. Taylor, "Shop Management," Trans. ASME, Vol. XXIV (June, 1903), pp. 1337-1480.

> the foreman and workmen, are shown by the rate-fixing department to be of paramount importance in obtaining the maximum output, and to require the most careful and systematic study and attention in order to insure uniformity and a fair and equal chance for each workman.[43]

It is here, with the introduction of the standardization of tools and equipment that Taylor continued to develop his concept of standards. He felt that standards in one aspect of shop management would logically necessitate standards for all phases of the factory. We will see later that this also included the standardization of costs in an accounting framework.

For the engineer, standards meant that all phases of the actual production process needed to be standardized. To management, the standardization meant that standard or expected levels of production by workmen could be assumed. Further, it was felt that the management would need to standardize and streamline their management methods, in terms of office procedure and personnel, in order to accommodate the changes that standardization in the factory brought about. For the accountant, standardization was the method by which he controlled all that was going on in the factory and office. He was able to predict what production output and subsequent costs would be. The entire process of standardization brought control to the factory and all its aspects.

---

[43] *Ibid.*, p. 1353.

C.B. Thompson noted that while Taylor was developing the practical aspects of scientific management he helped himself freely to the suggestions of Metcalfe[44] and incorporated them, with considerable modification, into his practice.[45] This provides some evidence that Taylor's contribution to accounting and bookkeeping directly was not completely original. His contribution "through scientific management" was original and will be discussed in Chapter V.

Motion Study

One concern of scientific management was the scientific determination of the most efficient way of conserving energy for heavy manual labor. Frank Gilbreth, one of Taylor's associates, was the pioneer in developing motion studies. His most famous work concerned itself with the art of bricklaying. Taylor's contribution was in minimizing muscular strain and utilizing human energy to the utmost. Instead of the workmen speeding up, which would result in fatigue, he had them rest at given intervals. Taylor's interest in motion study began in 1898 while

---

[44]Captain Henry Metcalfe, "The Shop Order System of Accounts," Trans. ASME, Vol. VII (1886), pp. 440-68, 475-88 and Captain Henry Metcalfe, The Cost of Manufactures and the Administration of Workshops Public and Private (New York: Wiley, 1885).

[45]C.B. Thompson, The Theory and Practice of Scientific Management, p. 187.

working at Bethlehem Steel. Through careful selection of his men, high pay for success and direction as to how the work should be done, Taylor was able to increase the amount of tons of pig iron loaded daily from 12 1/2 to 47 1/2.[46]

Selection of Workmen

This topic has already been mentioned briefly as incidental to the motivation of workmen. In "Shop Management," Taylor described his methods in use at the Symonds Rolling Machine Company. As a result of his careful selection of workmen on an inspection of machined parts at the plant, "thirty-five girls did the work formerly done by one hundred and twenty."[47]

Supplies

In order for work to be done most efficiently, necessary and standard tools and supplies must always be available. Workmen should never have to want because the supplies are not there before them. Also, tools must be in perfect condition when given to the workmen. Thus, under the Taylor system, tools were stored

---

[46]Drury, Scientific Management, p. 78.

[47]Taylor, "Shop Management," p. 1384.

in a well-organized system using mnemonic symbols[48] to minimize time spent in finding the proper tools for a job.

In general, scientific management involved an internal organizational readjustment by which the division of labor and specialization of skill were extended further than before. Taylor proposed in his concept of "functional management" to remove decisions, as much as is possible, from the workman's job. He believed that all decisions should be made in a planning department. His functional management concept became one of the more important developments in management of the time.

Summary

This was scientific management--a well-developed system for management. Significant strides were taken in large organizations during this period towards the advancement of managerial control and organizational effectiveness. As will be seen in the next chapter, this movement towards scientific management found a need for better cost information and developed a standard cost system to be integrated into the organization's management system.

---

[48]Taylor was not the first to use mnemonic symbols in this way. Metcalfe discussed their use in his Cost of Manufactures.

CHAPTER V

THE INTERACTION OF SCIENTIFIC MANAGEMENT AND COST ACCOUNTING (1900-1920)

The Need for Standard Costs

It is evident from previous discussion that estimates were basic to the scientific management system. The wage rate scheme was based on the setting of realistic production standards and the following through in the factory process. All factory operations, from equipment and supply maintenance to office procedures were standardized. This was necessary for the standardization system to be functional.

The accounting systems in these factories were seen as means of informing management and others of the costs of production. In order to set prices for a bid contract, the management found a need to be able to predetermine or estimate costs. Therefore, accounting also fell under the principle of standardization.

Thus, standard cost accounting is the logical consequence of scientific management. For scientific management to function properly, standard costs were needed. It can be seen in the accounting literature of the time (1900-1920) that few accountants understood or wrote about standard cost systems, unless they had been involved in a company where scientific management had been installed. Further, it will be shown that the accounting literature from 1900-1910 shows little acknowledgment of standard costs. With the Eastern Rate Case in 1910, scientific management ideas spread and more accounting literature can be seen referring to standards. The beginnings of sophistication and refinement in standard cost accounting techniques, appear most notably in the work of G. Charter Harrison from 1919 onward. The crude beginnings of standards in costing will be seen in the accounting literature of two distinct periods; 1900-1910 and 1911-1920. This accounting literature will show the effect of scientific management on the development of the standard cost system after 1911. In Chapter VI, it will be shown that an earlier and more direct impact in connection with Taylor's private consulting arrangements existed. The installation of the Taylor system into a manufacturing company required first that time-motion studies be conducted and then that standards be set with specific costs attached. This is basically how standard cost accounting developed under the Taylor system.

Although it can be shown that some early writers, such as H.M. Lane, compared actual costs to estimated costs, the estimated amount was not based on any scientific method. Time-motion studies and the Taylor system introduced the calculated estimate which set standards through accurate measurements. Before this system, estimates were a crude, unmeasured form of a standard. Obviously, the importance of the development of this actual-standard comparison can not be underrated.

This chapter shall generally follow chronological order, including all accounting literature deemed important, to show the impact of scientific management on the development of standard cost accounting.

The Turn of the Twentieth Century: The First Decade

Alexander Hamilton Church is considered one of the leading cost accountants at the turn of the century as well as a management systems innovator. The emphasis of his early works is on the establishment of burden rates (overhead costs), and takes little notice of cost estimates and standards. In discussing the integrative function of the organization or operations of the factory, Church speaks of the necessity of control and coordination concepts due to increased competition. He indicates that "everything should be the subject of forecast as to financial results,"[1] yet does not specify what form this "forecast" might take. He continues by stating that:

> the records of what did actually take place should be capable of comparison with what was intended to take place. Control then becomes a living reality.[2]

Church finds a relationship between control and comparison of standards with actual costs. This is extremely insightful for

---

[1]Alexander H. Church, "The Meaning of Commercial Organisation," Engineering Magazine, Vol. XIX (December, 1900), p. 397.

[2]Ibid.

his time, but Church does not specify what is meant by a standard, or more important, how the standard is to be determined.

In an extensive series of articles appearing in the Engineering Magazine, Church explains the concept of "establishment charges" as the "total difference between prime cost and inclusion cost of the product."[3] This concern for overhead cost determination and allocation was generally typical of the concerns of other accountants and cost authorities of that time. One of Church's major contributions to cost accounting was the introduction of the "production center" technique for allocating overhead expenses. He divided the factory into different production areas on the basis of floor space, number of employees, etc., and then apportioned expenses according to what each "center" produced on a machine hour rate basis.

Church's "production center" concept was "hailed as the greatest step forward which had been taken up to that time, and many cost authorities later drew heavily upon his suggestions."[4] Concern for standard costs had yet to begin.

---

[3]Alexander H. Church, "The Proper Distribution of Establishment Charges," Engineering Magazine, Vol. XX (July, 1901), p. 508.

[4]S. Paul Garner, Evolution of Cost Accounting to 1925 (Montgomery, Alabama: University of Alabama Press, 1954), p. 188.

Other Examples of Cost-Finding

Also in 1901, James Newton Gunn wrote about the importance of cost keeping. In addition, he acknowledged the need for some comparative basis of costs, estimated and actual. By comparative costs, he meant "between the costs of one period and another, and the costs of like articles as produced in different plants under control of the same corporation."[5] He acknowledged the importance of more accurate cost information for decision making, but did not forsee the use of estimates in any specific case.

As mentioned earlier, the emphasis during this period was on the determination of actual costs. In some cases, attempts were made at the standardization of factory operations for cost reduction. Writings about these systems usually illustrated the elaborate records that were kept and the forms used to avoid confusion by workmen. An excellent example of this is found in "A New Factory System" by Wilfred Bancroft. In this article he emphasized that:

> One of the most important points in cost reduction is to be sure that work will be done in exactly the manner that careful consideration has shown to be most advisable. To insure that no point in the predetermined method of machining the various pieces was overlooked, a service card was made out for each operation.[6]

---

[5]James Newton Gunn, "Cost Keeping; A Subject of Fundamental Importance," Engineering Magazine, Vol. XX (January, 1901), p. 706.

[6]Wilfred Bancroft, "A New Factory Cost Accounting System," American Machinist, July 24, 1902, p. 1048.

As with other articles at this time, Bancroft neither discusses the determination of the standard nor the use of the standard in some total cost accounting system.

In another example, Hugo Diemer's series of articles in Engineering Magazine were limited to a description of accurate cost keeping systems. He discussed a need for "careful classification of the particular items constituting the expense account under separate standing-order numbers" that "will enable the management to compare them from month to month from the cost department's summary of these orders."[7]

In another article, Diemer showed how product cost reductions could be affected by accurate cost keeping. In a description of the Cincinnati Milling Machine Company he claimed that the management of the company was "perfectly satisfied with the results in the greater output, and the reduction of the burden rate, to say nothing of the advantages of having accurate costs. . . ."[8]

Standard cost accounting techniques can be viewed as the ultimate in refinement and sophistication of the scientific management principle. Diemer acknowledged this when stating that the chief advantages of scientific management techniques

---

[7]Hugo Diemer, "Commercial Organization of the Machine Shop," Engineering Magazine, Vol. XIX (June, 1900), p. 347.

[8]Hugo Diemer, "Cost Finding Methods for Moderate-Sized Shops," Engineering Magazine, Vol. XXIV (January, 1903), p. 586.

were for cost reduction. Cost reduction was an important consequence of the differential rate scheme, but clearly not the chief result. Instead, standardization of work processes was the main result of the effects of this new wage scheme.

Karl Weber, in his work on American Standard cost accounting, referred to an article by Percy Longmuir as "the very earliest American work" on standard cost accounting.[9] He further asserted that "Longmuir suggests measuring the actual costs with carefully established standards. . . ."[10] Though this is true, Longmuir's standards were based on actual costs of the previous period, rather than on a more scientific and predetermined system of standards.

Longmuir states that "experience will readily give standard factors for each class of work,"[11] and continues to compare actual cost with a previous actual cost as a measure of performance. Obviously, this is substantially different than the determination of a standard based on time motion studies. Thus, with Longmuir's approach, the only information is how well performance compares with previous performance.

---

[9]Karl Weber, American Standard Cost Accounting: An Overview (Verlag P.G. Keller - Winterthur, 1960), p. 3. As translated by Joanne McKnight.

[10]Ibid., p. 4.

[11]Percy Longmuir, "Recording and Interpreting Foundry Costs," Engineering Magazine, Vol. XXIII (September, 1902), p. 890.

In one of the first books published on cost accounting in this early period. H.L.C. Hall directs himself both to the specifics of accurate cost keeping and to why accurate costs should be kept. His reasons for keeping accurate costs are for the reduction in wastes and product costs.

Through a hypothetical example he indicates a need for the comparison of previous product costs in determining a bid price. He concluded that "given an accurate and complete record of past performances along any definite lines it is usually safe to assume that future performances can be carried out at the same cost, or possibly less, always providing that the cost of labor and the prices of raw materials are the same."[12] This again indicates that cost accounting had not developed to the level which is common in what is known as standard cost accounting. He is not setting standards but rather just using past performance as a predictor for future performance.

By the middle of this first decade, 1900-1910, some writers began using the term standard costs, but no evidence links this with the concept developed by scientific management. D.C. Eggleston, a leading cost accountant of the time wrote several articles in the Journal of Accountancy concerning factory cost systems.

---

[12] H.L.C. Hall, Manufacturing Cost (Detroit: Book Keeper Publishing Company, 1904), p. 10.

In an early article,[13] he described a factory cost system in the cost-keeping tradition of the time. He discussed different methods for indirect cost determination, and included a supplementary rate system as one of these methods. In discussing how the supplementary rate allocates the idle time expense of machinery on a percentage basis, he mentioned the term standard cost and implied a comparison of various costs of production, but a thorough discussion of standards, how they are used, or how they are set was not included.[14]

Two years later he further explained, and perhaps refined, his concept of standard costs. He saw "standard leading rates" as representative of the average "rate of normal expense." While he described standard rates as averages, he also discussed a change in the rates due to: (a) Change in speed or method of machines; (b) Change in the distribution of idle machine time; (c) Change in prices of supplies, etc.[15] This seems to indicate some movement at least, towards the standard cost system but the cost-keeping function was still primary. Further, he does not make the "standard loading rates" operational by discussing their measurement.

---

[13]D.C. Eggleston, "A System of Factory Cost Accounting," Journal of Accountancy, Vol. III, No. 2 (December, 1906), p. 115.

[14]Ibid., p. 121.

[15]D.C. Eggleston, "Factory Cost Accounting," Businessman's Magazine, January, 1908, p. 99.

John Whitmore

Both Garner and Solomons consider John Whitmore's lecture at the New York University School of Commerce in 1908 to be the clearest explanation of standard costing until that time.[16] Whitmore demonstrated a good conception of what standard costing should be, but gave no indication of its use by himself or others in professional accounting. He stated that:

> It is possible to carry the application of the principle distinguishing between proper and improper cost so far as to use calculations of proper and improper costs, and then to direct the cost accounting to showing the variations of actual from calculated costs. This involves the setting up of complete standards for quality in materials and efficiency in working, and is not to be confused with estimates of probable cost which are arrived at by any superficial method, or except with the idea of continuously testing actual and calculated costs with each other.[17]

Whitmore saw a need for the consideration of changes, failure or advancement, in the setting of standards. He used improper costs as those "blunders or accidents" which could not be applied to the product cost and should not be a part of the standard (i.e., unused factory capacity).[18] He used standards

---

[16] S. Paul Garner, Cost Accounting to 1925, p. 134. David Solomons, "The Historical Development of Costing," in Studies in Cost Analysis, edited by David Solomons (Homewood, Illinois: Richard D. Irwin, Inc., 1953), p. 40.

[17] John Whitmore, "Shoe Factory Cost Accounts," Journal of Accountancy, Vol. VI (May, 1908), p. 14.

[18] Ibid., p. 14.

in labor through the use of a "Labor Cost Sheet." This form covered all operations of work and priced each operation on piece rate and day rate (average of wage to amount produced) basis. He then compared these "cost sheets" to actual differences in labor expense due to product variation. Though sophisticated in some ways, this type of standard is not akin to the standardization within scientific management. That movement, through the use of time study, determined what could and should be produced. Whitmore, on the other hand, does not indicate how these "standards" are determined or specifically how they are to be used. (He does specify, though, that the standards are not the result of spurious averages of day rates and piece rates.)[19] He specifies, however, that the standards are to be used in the determination of the differential wage rate. This, of course, is the same wage rate scheme proposed by Taylor thirteen years earlier in "A Piece Rate System." Thus, one of the reasons that Whitmore's contribution cannot be considered to be the major contribution of the time is his lack of specification on the methods for the determination of standards.

Emerson's Concept of Standards

Harrington Emerson, in a series of articles entitled "Efficiency as a Basis for Operations," dealt with the essence of

---

19*Ibid.*, p. 24.

standard costing. His stress on efficiency led him to develop "Comparison of Costs" statements based on actual vs. "realizable" standard amounts.[20] He attempted to determine the per cent of efficiency, and then maximize it through changes in the method and operation of doing work.

In an organizational sense, Emerson saw inefficiency as common to all organizations. To reduce inefficiency, an organization must have a line and staff system in operation. Thus, the staff sets up the standards so that the line is able to work more efficiently.[21]

Emerson equates the standard with the ideal, which is similar to Taylor's time motion study method. In one specific case, surveys were taken to determine the standard.

> In the third survey a number of labor assays or audits determined the relation between what men were actually doing and what they should do; the fourth survey showed as to a few operations in the relation between current costs and standard costs.[22]

It is somewhat unclear from this passage whether "standards" and "what should be" can be equated. Solomons, in his essay on the development of costing, criticizes Emerson for just this kind of

---

[20]Harrington Emerson, "Efficiency As a Basis for Operation," Engineering Magazine, Vol. XXXV, No. 4 (July, 1908), p. 534.

[21]Harrington Emerson, "Efficiency As a Basis for Operation," Engineering Magazine, Vol. XXXVI, No. 2 (November, 1908), p. 170.

[22]Ibid., p. 172.

ambiguity. Further, Emerson does not describe how the standard costs are to be determined and this determination is considered to be an integral part of the standard cost system. But, even with these criticisms, Emerson's contribution to standard costing will be seen to be as major as that of Taylor's.

In explaining the chart below, Emerson defined the standard as "theoretically predetermined by standardizing not the cost of work, but the efficiency of men, of machines and of methods."[23]

EXHIBIT 3

DEPARTMENT F.[24]

Statement of Condition for 12 Months Preceeding June 30 on Basis of Standard Volume of Output.

Costs per Hour.

	Actual.	Standard.	Reduction.
Direct wages	$36.93	$27.77	25 per cent.
Overhead or indirect expenses..	18.98	11.11	41.5 percent.
Machine expenses	48.94	29.17	40 per cent.
Totals	$104.85	$68.05	35.1 per cent.

Total Costs per Annum.

Direct	$99,794	$75,000	$24,794
Overhead	51,255	30,000	21,255
Machine expenses	117,470	70,000	47,470
Totals	$268,519	$175,000	$ 93,519

---

[23] Ibid., p. 174.

[24] Ibid., p. 173.

As can be readily seen, Exhibit 3 above is more advanced than other writings of the time, though Taylor and others did prepare statements like this in private consulting arrangements as will be seen in Chapter VI. Emerson's uses of the word "standard" has been seen before in the writings of others, but he appears to be the first one to use "pre-determined" in relation to the standard. And more importantly, his discussion seems to indicate a concept close to that which we use today.

In one of the series of articles, Emerson discussed the theory of cost accounting. He stated that actual costs must be divided into standard costs and preventable wastes. These standard costs must always be pre-determined and based on what "real" costs might be. The method of accounting Emerson proposed ascertained costs before the work was undertaken, which is substantially different than the previous method of ascertaining costs after the work is finished.[25] This predetermination process is based on "scientific certainties modified by experience."[26] It should be seen that these advances moved cost accounting during this period close to the standard cost system we use today.

The role of the "efficiency engineer" was to reduce wastes. Through the use of the predetermined standard he could determine

---

[25]Harrington Emerson, "Efficiency As a Basis for Operations," Engineering Magazine, Vol. XXXVI, No. 3 (December, 1908), p. 336.

[26]Ibid., p. 337.

the amount of waste by subtracting the standard cost from the actual. He then proceeded to eliminate these wastes and revise the standard costs "since the basic elements of costs, materials, services and operations are not constant in value."[27]

Further Examples of Standards in Operation

In J.L. Nicholson's first book,[28] he discussed a good system of cost accounting that included estimated costs and comparisons of the actual with the estimated. He did not, however, discuss how the estimate was to be made, which has been mentioned about almost every other author discussed. We can assume that other estimates were made by "superficial methods" as Whitmore suggested.[29] Obviously, the important contributions of both the Taylor system and the Emerson system were the development of ways to measure and to set standards.

Taylor, Gilbreth (time motion studies) and Emerson (efficiency system) developed the methods by which standards were set. They were engineers and, as stated before, accounting advancements at this time came from the engineers whose responsibilities were far greater than developing machinery and functional

---

[27] Ibid., p. 342.

[28] J.L. Nicholson, Factory Organization and Costs (New York: Kohl Technical Publishing Company, 1909).

[29] Whitmore, "Shoe Factory Cost Accounts," p. 14.

work space conditions. The engineers needed standards for their job of systemizing the entire work experience, and had the capability and experience needed to develop and use these standards. Frederick Taylor needed standards to develop "a fair days work" for his differential wage rate system. Before the advent of wage rate schemes as the "solution" to inefficiency and the "wages problem," standardization was not considered necessary. The need to measure and set accurate predetermined standard costs grew out of the "wages problem" solution of the engineers.

Nicholson and others used very crude estimates. These estimates were generally rough calculations of previous costs of production with no time studies and no estimates of standard cost or reasons for variances from that standard. Nicholson attempted to obtain these rough estimates, but did not need the systematic accurate numbers which Taylor used since this was not an integral part of his system. These cost estimates were an added flair of supposed sophistication by the accountant. Taylor's entire system relied on accurate wage standards; inaccuracy would result in underpaid workers who would quit from dissatisfaction, or overpaid workers who would not work up to some efficient level. Both situations were undesirable, and therefore well set standards were the only answer.

Cost accountants' estimates and standard setting procedures were, for the most part, poor. Further, the important point remains that well set standards did not come about until Taylor. Estimates are of little value if not accurately determined on some scientific or factual basis, thus Nicholson and others did not have a standard cost system (as defined in Chapter I).

Another clear explanation of how cost estimates are made is found in a book by Leslie Unckless[30] which was written for the practical application of costing methods rather than for theoretical purposes. One can easily distinguish between the theoreticians and practitioners. Thus, Whitmore, Church, Hall, Longmuir, and others wrote theoretical treatises dealing for the most part in abstractions. This abstraction level is a causal factor in their inadequate understanding of standard costs. Eggleston, Nicholson, and Diemer, on the other hand, wrote from practical experiences for practitioners (managers and engineers). The practical applications often do not make use of the appropriate concept of standard costing, but a methodology and more concrete conclusions can be made from their misconceptions or conceptions of the term.

Unckless gives a clear explanation of how cost estimates are made so that the "probable cost" of a manufactured good could be determined before the production process began. In order to develop this predetermined estimate he used an "Estimate and

---

[30]Leslie Unckless, How to Find Manufacturing Costs and Selling Costs (Detroit: Modern Methods Publishing Company, 1909).

Cost Sheet." It categorically disallowed the use of guesswork as a means of making the estimate. The estimate "is auxiliary to the cost and while not of equal importance perhaps, it yet serves as a check in costs."[31] When making the estimate, he divided the expense into Material, Labor, and Expense (overhead). But, his methods can best be described as educated guesswork, for when it comes to estimating the labor expense, he maintains that those costs should be obtained from the foreman or superintendent, "since they are best fitted to furnish information of that kind."[32]

Summary of the First Decade

An interesting phenomenon for the historian to follow is the development in thought of an individual or group through time. In one of his later works, Church[33] indicated some change in thought partly due to the influence of Harrington Emerson. Although Church's main concern was still with the allocation of overhead expenses, he recognized the possible uses of standards. He further recognized that one of the more important uses of actual costs is for comparative purposes with estimates.[34]

---

[31] Ibid., pp. 22-23.

[32] Ibid., p. 24.

[33] Alexander Hamilton Church, Production Factors in Cost Accounting and Works Management (New York: The Engineering Magazine Press, 1910).

[34] Ibid., p. 38.

The first decade of the twentieth century showed a lack of clear understanding of the composition of a standard cost system. It has been shown, though, that Emerson, who was an efficiency engineer and had developed a parallel system to Taylor's, had the clearest conception about standard cost of all the "accountants" discussed thus far. Emerson was able to place the accounting function within the total systems framework of the organization, which is important in realizing his achievements in standard costing. It would be reckless to infer that only efficiency experts made use of and understood standard costing techniques. But, there is some indication in this early decade and more in the later decade, in terms of the literature, that acquaintance with scientific management techniques aided in understanding standards and their application in industry. It can be seen that only the efficiency and scientific management proponents contributed widely to the development and implementation of standards and standard costing systems. (This will be further discussed in the section on <u>The Effects of Scientific Management</u>, later in this chapter.)

As is apparent from the first part of this chapter, relatively little was written on cost accounting pertaining to standard cost systems. At this period in cost accounting development, accountants and engineers interested in cost accounting were mainly concerned with the distribution of overhead expenses, especially problems of interest, rent, and depreciation allocations to product costs.

The Second Decade

In Karl Weber's book on standard costing, Harrington Emerson is credited with being the "father" of standard cost accounting. Though the importance of Harrington Emerson's contribution is not questioned, Weber relies too heavily on Solomons' work to state a truly convincing case. Solomons lays stress on the ambiguities of Emerson's terminology and his lack of applications.[35] After agreeing with Solomons criticism, Weber then goes on to prove the opposite: that Emerson really did understand his concepts and knew how to apply them.[36]

Emerson's Standard Cost System

It is the opinion of this author that Emerson's two books,[37] one of which was a compilation and rewording of this article series

---

[35]David Solomons, "The Historical Development of Costing," in David Solomons, ed., Studies in Cost Analysis (Homewood, Illinois: Richard D. Irwin, 1968), p. 41.

[36]Weber, American Cost Accounting: An Overview, p. 10.

[37]Harrington Emerson, Efficiency As a Basis for Operation and Wages (New York: Engineering Magazine Company, 1912). The Twelve Principles of Efficiency (New York: John R. Dunlap, 1911).

in Engineering Magazine (1908-1909) and the other on his principles of efficiency, clarify any of the shortcomings that were possibly attributable to his earlier work.

In Efficiency as a Basis for Operation and Wages Emerson presents a formula which indicates the relationship between actual and standard costs. It is a concise formula stated as:

$$\text{Actual Cost} = \frac{Q}{Eq.}\left[\frac{P}{EP} + \frac{Bp}{Ebp}\right] + \frac{T}{Et}\left[\frac{W}{Ew} + \frac{Bw}{Ebw}\right] + \frac{T'}{Et'}\left[\frac{R}{Er} + \frac{Br}{Ebr}\right]$$

Q = Standard Quantity of Materials

P = Standard Price per unit of Quantity

Bp = Standard Burden on standard price

T = Standard time of labor

W = Standard rate of wages per hour

Bw = Standard Burden on wage rate

T' = Standard time for equipment or machine

R = Standard rate of machine charge

Br = Standard burden on machine rate

E = Efficiency of each of the nine items[38]

Emerson illustrates this concept of standards through a hypothetical case of railroad operations.[39]

---

[38]As cited in Weber, American Cost Accounting: An Overview, p. 10.

[39]The example given is adapted from Emerson, Twelve Principles of Efficiency, pp. 213-14.

$$\underset{C}{\underset{\$2,755}{\text{Total cost}}} = \underset{M}{\underset{\$524}{\text{Material}}} + \underset{S}{\underset{\$1,021}{\text{Personal Service}}} + \underset{I}{\underset{\$1,210}{\text{Investment Charges}}}$$

Equating this with present day terminology, "Personal Service" is labor and "Investment Charges" is overhead. After a certain amount of investigation, it becomes apparent that "the same general result" can be accomplished with less costs. Thus the standard cost formula derived is:

$$\underset{\$1750}{\text{C Standard}} = \underset{\$350}{M} + \underset{\$780}{S} + \underset{\$600}{I}$$

The efficiency ratio of the whole operation is:

$$\frac{\text{C standard}}{\text{C actual}} = \frac{\$1,750}{\$2,755} = 63.5 \text{ per cent} = \text{Total Efficiency (E)}$$

Thus:

$$\frac{\text{Material Cost standard}}{\text{Material cost actual}} = \frac{\$\ 370}{\$\ 524} = 70.6\% = \text{Material efficiency}$$

$$\frac{\text{Labor cost standard}}{\text{Labor cost actual}} = \frac{\$\ 780}{\$1,021} = 76.4\% = \text{Service efficiency}$$

$$\frac{\text{Investment cost standard}}{\text{Investment cost actual}} = \frac{\$\ 600}{\$1,210} = 49.6\% = \text{Investment efficiency}$$

Actual costs are then stated in terms of standard cost and of efficiency:

$$\text{Total actual cost} = \frac{\text{Total Standard cost}}{\text{Total Efficiency}} = \frac{\$1,750}{63.5} = \$2,755$$

$$\text{Total Actual Cost} = \frac{\text{Standard Cost of Material}}{\text{Material Efficiency}} + \frac{\text{Standard Cost of Service}}{\text{Service Efficiency}} + \frac{\text{Standard Cost of Investment}}{\text{Investment Efficiency}}$$

$$\text{Total actual cost} = \frac{\$\ 370}{70.6\%} + \frac{\$\ 780}{76.4\%} + \frac{\$\ 600}{49.6\%} = \$2,755$$

This long example clearly shows the sophistication in Emerson's thinking. He understood and could apply his standard cost concepts and appears to be the first one to develop some concept of variances.

Though the comparison of actual and standard costs as we know it today is significantly different than Emerson's calculation of percent of efficiency, similarities can be seen. Using the example above, today we would determine, for example, a material cost variance as follows:

Material cost actual - Material cost standard = (Un)favorable Material cost variance.

$524 - $370 = ($154)

(Given sufficient information, we could further isolate rate and efficiency variances, yield and mix variances, etc.) The expression of a $154 unfavorable material cost variance and the expression of a material efficiency of only 70.6% yield the same implication. Though they are expressed in different terms, both expressions indicate operating at less than standard performance.

To further illustrate his concepts, Emerson states:

> If we know in advance the standard or theoretical costs, if we know the current efficiencies, we can predetermine actual costs. What we all desire is to make the industrial machine as efficient as possible, to bring efficiencies up to 100 per cent . . . ."[40]

---

[40]*Ibid.*, p. 215.

The Effects of Scientific Management

The leading engineering and accounting journals contained articles dealing with cost accounting and its close association with scientific management principles. In an article by Louis D. Brandeis in the Journal of Accountancy.[41] Brandeis makes a strong case for scientific management, although he doesn't talk about cost accounting at all. An article by Taylor describing his management system also appeared in this journal.[42] The Journal of Accountancy, the leading accounting journal of the time, apparently recognized the importance of scientific management to the accounting profession, by including these articles in their journal.

In both the Engineering Magazine and the Transactions of the American Society of Mechanical Engineers, recognition is clearly given to the importance of Taylor's cost methods, the need for standard costing, and the relation of scientific management to cost accounting. Sterling Bunnell, though primarily concerned with overhead expense allocations, recognizes the need for "principles of estimation correctly . . . ."[43] He considers his

---

[41]Louis D. Brandeis, "The New Conception of Industrial Efficiency," Journal of Accountancy, May, 1911.

[42]Frederick Taylor, "Principles and Methods of Scientific Management," Journal of Accountancy, June, July, 1911, pp. 117-24, 181-88.

[43]Sterling Bunnell, "Expense Burden: It's Incidence and Distribution," Trans. ASME, Vol. XXXI (1911), p. 535.

method of overhead allocation as providing for a comparison of actual expense "with the schedule or budget as a standard."[44] The most interesting part of Bunnell's article is the discussion of it by such a notable scientific management proponent as H.K. Hathaway. Hathaway provides a fusion point for these two systems, cost accounting and scientific management, when he concurs that Bunnell's method "is essentially that developed under the Taylor system of management . . . ."[45]

In a different article, Bunnell clearly established the debt that the standard cost system owes to scientific management. He argued that in the determination of the ratio of efficiency, "the standard quantity, time, or cost of the work, as set forth by Mr. Taylor and his associates"[46] must be considered to be the denominators of that ratio with actual cost as the numerator.

Much of standard cost information, today, is for internal control and as an aid to managerial decision making. In 1912, Benjamin A. Franklin addressed himself to these issues. Managers already knew something about their costs, but didn't know whether these were the "right" costs. Thus, he proposed the use of standard costs, with consideration of variances and implicit cost standard

---

[44] Ibid., p. 536.

[45] Ibid., p. 551.

[46] Sterling Bunnell, "Are Profits a Proper Measure of Efficiency?" Iron Age, December 5, 1912, p. 1318.

changes as vital to the understanding of costs. The ability "to figure estimates or predictions of cost from a standard under varying conditions gauges the comprehension of the meaning and value of practical costs."[47]

In "The Relation of Detailed Planning and the Cost of Production" by C.A. Harrington, the "detailed planning of work" under the scientific management system is expounded. Planning is recognized here as essential to the continued growth and success of any organization. One of the basics of this scientific planning system is an accounting system of comparative costs. "This comparison will be easily afforded by the concern which manufactures standard articles whose cost is available prior to the introduction of our system."[48] Again we find the logical connection of standard costs with scientific management.

The subject of variances in railroad efficiency arose in an attempt to standardize railroad records and decrease wastes. F. Lincoln Hutchins saw a need for "systematic statistical methods" that gave a true indication of operation costs. To this end he felt that standards were needed to determine those variances or

---

[47]Benjamin A. Franklin, "Cost Methods That Give the Executive Control of His Business," Engineering Magazine, Vol. XLIII, p. 578.

[48]C.A. Harrington, "The Relation of Detailed Planning and the Cost of Production," Engineering Magazine, June, 1913, p. 355.

amounts of wastes, if efficiency was to be increased. But, Hutchins didn't care whether the standard was accurate so long as it provided some "bench mark" to determine where and what the inefficiencies were.[49]

Solomons suggests that from 1912 on there was a change in emphasis from "the ascertainment of what it costs to make something to the control of what it costs to carry out an industrial process or function."[50] Solomons has made an extremely important point here, but it needs to be extended. With the establishment and popularization of scientific management from 1911 on, standard costs as a basic element in this system no longer were seen as important goals to strive for in both accounting development and production efficiency. What did become important then is the tool, production control, which was used as the means to achieve maximum efficiency at the least cost. Scovell stated this concept clearly:

> I want to point out that good cost accounting is a help to efficient management, not only as it traces and records values but also as it may be made a powerful agent for production control. From my experience in professional service for industrial plants, I emphasize more and more the practical value of this second aspect of the work.[51]

---

[49]F. Lincoln Hutchins, "A Practical Plan for Standardizing Railroad Records," Engineering Magazine, Vol. XLV (August, 1913).

[50]Solomons, "The Historical Development of Costing," p. 46.

[51]Clinton H. Scovell, "Cost Accounting Practice, With Special Reference to Machine Hour Rate," Journal of Accountancy, January, 1914, p. 16.

The close connection between standard cost accounting and cost control in this later period was also acknowledged by Armstrong.[52] In discussing the importance of cost accounting in the railroads, Armstrong stated that one of the most important functions of cost accounting is to enable the executive to make decisions on a more factual basis. The entire article seems to be based on a pre-acknowledgment that "standards" were the accepted method of cost determination. Written in 1920, this article shows a significant change from the 1900-1910 period, about the necessity of standard costs.

H.L. Gantt, one of the leaders in the scientific management movement, wrote articles recognizing the importance of standard cost in the production process. He saw one of the most important duties of the "cost keeper" as providing the manager with information to compare "what has been done with what should have been done." He goes on to say, "costs are valuable only as comparisons, and comparisons are of little value unless we have a standard, which it is the function of the engineer to set."[54] Gantt also indicates

---

[52]George Armstrong, "Cost Accounting--The Key to Cost Control," Railway Mechanical Engineer, June, 1920.

[53]H.L. Gantt, "The Relation Between Costs and Production," The Gas Engine, Vol. XVIII (October, 1916), p. 524.

[54]H.L. Gantt, "Production and Sales," The Engineering Magazine, January, 1916, p. 599.

that cost accounting must be for the control of costs rather than only cost-finding or cost-keeping.

The End of the Second Decade: G. Charter Harrison

The level of sophistication in standard costing techniques reached a high point in 1920 with the contribution of G. Charter Harrison. Harrison distinctly places the debt for the development of costing on the scientific management movement. "Notably, Frederick W. Taylor and Harrington Emerson developed cost work, and wrote emphasizing the place of importance that costs occupy in the general scheme of management in industry."[55] Harrison acknowledged an exceedingly high debt to Emerson, which in part can be explained by some personal contact they had together in 1909. Harrison distinguishes between the contributions of Emerson and Taylor. To Taylor he attributes the pioneering effort in the development of scientific management; but to Emerson he attributes the application of scientific management to other aspects of life. The results of Emerson's work "represent a revolution in our attitude toward life in general as well as industrially."[56]

Harrison seemed surprised that little thought had been given by cost accountants to their relationship with the

---

[55] G. Charter Harrison, Cost Accounting to Aid Production (New York: Engineering Magazine, 1921), p. iv.

[56] G. Charter Harrison, "Scientific Basis for Cost Accounting," Industrial Management, Vol. LIX, No. 3, p. 238.

scientific management school. It is an obvious fact to him:

> It seems in fact rather remarkable to the writer that considering the immense amount of time which has been devoted to cost accounting by many intelligent men, that in a subject so obviously akin to mathematical science so little attempt has apparently been made to determine whether the accepted methods conform to the recognized standards of scientific work.[57]

One of Harrison's greatest accomplishments was his sophisticated use of cost variances. He divided cost variance analysis into the following specific ratios:

1. The variation in total.
2. The variation due to the revision of the standard.
3. The variation due to the use of an alternate standard.
4. The variation in cost resulting from the number of working days in the month being more or less than the number of working days in the standard month used as a basis for figuring standard costs.
5. The variation in cost owing to idle time.
6. The variation due to the production per day or hour being more or less than standard.
7. The variation due to fluctuations in the rate of pay.
8. The variation due to fluctuations in the hours worked as compared with standard.
9. The variation due to differences between the actual and standard price paid for material.
10. The variation in the quantity of material used.
11. The variation in the price of service such as power, light, etc.
12. The variation in the quantity of service consumed.
13. The variation in expense.[58]

He sees the necessity of cost variance analysis for cost control purposes. In some ways, it might even be said that the variance breakdown above is more complete than is in common use today.

---

[57] *Ibid.*, p. 238.

[58] *Ibid.*, p. 239.

Harrison applies Taylor's management by exception to cost accounting methods. This involves "firstly the comparisons of all expenses with standards and secondly the analysis of variations from standard as to the causes underlying variations.[59]

In reviewing the impact of Harrison on standard cost accounting development, Solomon's statement that Harrison developed the first complete standard cost system "known to exist" is quite correct.[60]

Summary

Thus in this span of 20 years we have moved from cost-keeping and cost-finding for accurate results to a highly sophisticated standard cost system for control purposes. It is evident from the literature presented here that the scientific management movement provided conditions for the rapid development of standard costing. It is further evident that standard costs were a necessary and integral part of the scientific management system.

---

[60]Solomons, "The Historical Development of Costing," p. 46.

CHAPTER VI

SOME SPECIFIC APPLICATIONS OF STANDARD COSTING

Taylor's Impact on Standard Cost Accounting

In Chapter IV, the dissemination of information concerning scientific management was discussed. In Chapter V, it was shown through published literature of the period of 1900-1920 that scientific management had an important and direct effect on the development of the standard cost system. Further, it was shown that this effect was causal, rather than random, due to the requirements of scientific management in its application in industry. The works of Taylor and Emerson were shown to be the earliest accounts of complete standard cost systems. But, an integral part of this study is a discussion of all available and relevant material concerning the interaction of scientific management and standard cost accounting in business organizations. As suggested earlier, most of this material is from the Taylor collection at Stevens Institute of Technology. It documents the assertion that standards were in use in organizations prior to the published articles in the accounting and engineering journals and the general popularization of scientific management. Most of this use will be seen to have emanated from the consulting engagements of Frederick Taylor.

The Taylor collection contains numerous relevant documents which demonstrate the use of standard cost principles in companies whose systems Taylor installed. As stated earlier, letters were sent to all companies still in existence known to have used the Taylor system in an attempt to obtain additional original records. No companies were able to supply these records due to the destruction of the records. (See Appendix B) Thus, this chapter will discuss all available relevant materials on the actual installation of scientific management in organizations with special emphasis on its effect on standard costing techniques.

Frederick Taylor was, by profession, a mechanical engineer. The system he developed, often referred to as the Taylor system, was an attempt to systematize, organize and standardize all methods of operation in manufacturing concerns. His system was first developed as a response to the inefficiencies of production that he observed while employed at Midvale Steel Company. He attempted to increase labor production and the quality of production through the application of time motion studies to the work process. Eventually, his system encompassed all phases of company operations. It was thus necessary for Taylor to develop a cost system that would reflect his standardized management system. For his wage plans to work effectively, accurate cost-keeping was necessary along with a predetermined standard to be compared with actual costs and then to determine any variances.

Taylor had little knowledge of accounting and an aversion to commercial figuring.[1] In 1893, Taylor wrote to William D. Basley, a professional accountant employed with the Manufacturing Investment Company, making some inquiries on accounting procedures. Basley replied in a letter to Taylor, July 12, 1893, outlining the principles of a general accounting system. Basley dealt mainly with the General Ledger and with subsidiary ledgers.[2] This was one of Taylor's first contacts with accounting concepts.

In a treatise, "Bookkeeping Under the Taylor System," Taylor acknowledged the need for accounts which reflect "Internal Transactions." "For instance; it is desirable to know just what each class of goods which we manufacture costs us each month, so as to note improvements or the reverse, and it is also desirable to locate the cause of improvement and to analyze the elements that go to make up our cost."[3] This indicates the earliest recognition by Taylor of the needs for internal control and the control of product costs. This later evolved into his refined

---

[1]Frank B. Copley, Frederick W. Taylor (New York: Augustus M. Kelley, 1923), Vol. I, p. 363.

[2]Letter from William D. Basley to Frederick Taylor, Madison, Maine, July 12, 1893. It should be noted that all letters referred to in this chapter are from the Frederick Winslow Taylor Collection at Stevens Institute of Technology, Hoboken, New Jersey and all further footnotes refer to that collection.

[3]F.W. Taylor, "Bookkeeping Under the Taylor System," 1893. (from F.W. Taylor Collection, Stevens Institute of Technology, Hoboken, New Jersey - Unpublished), p. 9.

system of standards generally and cost standards specifically. Through the use of "internal accounts" "we can find the exact source of all losses or gains."[4] He further seems to be moving towards a concept of the comparison of actual and standard and the computation of a variance. This early work was the beginning of his involvement with standard costing concepts.

Further, while managing a pulp and paper mill in Appleton, Wisconsin, for the Manufacturing Investment Company, Taylor concerned himself with the costs of using a digestor (a machine used for cooking cords of cut wood down into finer material to be used for manufacturing paper). In his treatise "Cost of Emptying and Filling a Digestor," Taylor discussed the experiment where he observed different work groupings in order to determine a most efficient or least cost method. He developed a comparative statement that showed "the time in filling and emptying of digestors in the Months of March, April, May, June, July, and August '92."[5] This statement was used "as a check against the observations to be used as a basis for prior work rates."[6]

---

[4]Ibid., p. 10.

[5]F.W. Taylor, "Cost of Emptying and Filling a Digestor," Appleton, Wisconsin, November 7, 1892. (Unpublished manuscript from F.W. Taylor Collection, Stevens Institute of Technology, Hoboken, New Jersey), p. 15.

[6]Ibid., p. 15.

With this short introduction to some of Taylor's early attempts at standardization and move toward standard costing, we now move to the discussion of companies that installed the Taylor system. The length of each discussion is primarily determined by the amount of available records. Each shows Taylor's influence on the development of the standard cost system.

The Midvale Steel Company

Midvale Steel processed iron into steel and produced specialized machinery for its clients on an individual order basis. The company was reorganized in 1872 under the presidency of William Sellers, who was also the head of William Sellers and Company, a closely associated manufacturing company. "It should be borne in mind that during most of Taylor's engagement with the Midvale Steel Co., William Sellers was president both of that company and the company bearing his name, and that the relations of the two companies during that period were not cordial."[7]
In 1875, Midvale became the first American Company to receive an order for gun forgings from the U.S. Navy, Department of Ordnance. This was the start of a large amount of government business for Midvale.

7Carl G. Barth, "A Brief Description of the Eight Large Gray Canvas Covered Books of Taylor's Memorabilia," (unpublished, 1933), p. 5.

> In 1881, when the Navy's Ordnance Bureau invited fifteen American Steel Manufacturers to submit proposals for forgings for six inch all steel guns, Midvale was the only plant that could undertake the work; for it alone had developed a complete system of experimentation and of records.[8]

This advance system of experimentation and records was the application of Taylor's early system of time study and standardization to the works of Midvale Steel. As discussed previously, the impetus for Taylor's system came at Midvale Steel Company, where Taylor attempted to get higher wages for the workers in concert with increased production output. To this end he introduced elementary time studies that essentially began the cycle of standardization. Standard time periods set for a task to be completed led to standard wage rates for that task, which eventually led to a standard cost for each item to be produced.

One of the earliest forms developed by Taylor is "Observation of Hand Work on Machine Tools."[9] The form contains comments by Taylor as to how the form is to be filled out and to what end. Taylor describes the form: "This blank will show either the setting and unsetting, or the re-setting of a job, even the shifting of clamps being considered a re-setting."[10]

---

[8]Copley, <u>Frederick W. Taylor</u>, Vol. I, p. 114.

[9]Observations of Hand Work on Machine Tools, Midvale Steel, 1882 (F.W. Taylor Collection, Stevens Institute of Technology, Hoboken, New Jersey).

[10]<u>Ibid</u>.

The significance of this form is that it compares actual and standard times for a given operations. Thus, the "Actual Time of Setting Work" is compared to the "Setting Work Should Have Taken" in total time and in each phase of setting work. Space is provided for explanations of delays in performing a task, so as to improve the work process to the highest standard attainable. The logical consequence of the established time standard was the determination of related cost. Today, we can identify these concepts as those used in standard cost accounting in the computation of variances.

In a Rate Table (Exhibit 4) prepared in February, 1886, the rate is broken down to minutes starting with 1/2 minute. It was the task of the Rate Setting Department to establish those tables. It provided information as to the cost of performing a job, no matter how small. Barth refers to this also as an estimating procedure which "was the beginning of his (Taylor's) final Planning Department with its numerous functions."[11]

The close association of the Midvale Steel and the William Sellers Company is found in a review by Taylor of the cost system in use at the works of William Sellers and Co. Taylor reviews the procedure, criticizes it and finally expounds on the superiority of his own system. The method of William Sellers and Co. was:

---

[11] Barth, "Eight Large Gray Canvas Covered Books," p. 5.

EXHIBIT 4

Min	.25	.30	.35	.40	.45	.50	.55	.60	.65	.70	.75	.80	.85
½	.02	.03	.03	.03	.04	.04	.05	.05	.05	.06	.06	.07	.07
1	.042	.050	.058	.067	.075	.083	.092	.100	.108	.117	.125	.133	.142
2	.08	.10	.12	.13	.15	.17	.18	.20	.22	.23	.25	.27	.28
3	.13	.15	.18	.20	.23	.25	.28	.30	.33	.35	.38	.40	.42
4	.17	.20	.23	.27	.30	.33	.27	.40	.43	.47	.50	.53	.57
5	.21	.25	.29	.33	.38	.42	.46	.50	.54	.58	.63	.67	.71
6	.25	.30	.35	.40	.45	.50	.55	.60	.65	.70	.75	.80	.85
7	.29	.35	.41	.47	.53	.58	.64	.70	.76	.82	.88	.93	.97
8	.33	.40	.47	.53	.60	.67	.73	.80	.87	.93	1.00	1.07	1.13
9	.38	.45	.53	.60	.68	.75	.83	.90	.98	1.05	1.13	1.20	1.28
10	.42	.50	.58	.67	.75	.83	.92	1.00	1.08	1.17	1.25	1.33	1.42
11	.46	.55	.64	.73	.83	.92	1.01	1.10	1.19	1.28	1.28	1.47	1.56
12	.50	.60	.70	.80	.90	1.00	1.10	1.20	1.30	1.40	1.50	1.60	1.70
13	.54	.65	.76	.87	.98	1.08	1.19	1.30	1.41	1.52	1.63	1.73	1.84
14	.58	.70	.82	.93	1.05	1.17	1.28	1.40	1.52	1.63	1.75	1.87	1.98
15	.63	.75	.88	1.00	1.13	1.25	1.38	1.50	1.63	1.75	1.88	2.00	2.13
16	.67	.80	.93	1.07	1.20	1.33	1.47	1.60	1.73	1.87	2.00	2.13	2.27
17	.71	.85	.99	1.13	1.28	1.42	1.56	1.70	1.84	1.98	2.13	2.27	2.41
18	.75	.90	1.05	1.20	1.35	1.50	1.65	1.80	1.95	2.10	2.25	2.40	2.55
19	.79	.95	1.11	1.27	1.43	1.58	1.74	1.90	2.06	2.22	2.38	2.53	2.69
20	.83	1.00	1.17	1.33	1.50	1.67	1.83	2.00	2.17	2.33	2.50	2.67	2.83
21	.88	1.05	1.23	1.40	1.58	1.75	1.93	2.10	2.28	2.45	2.63	2.80	2.98
22	.92	1.10	1.28	1.47	1.65	1.83	2.02	2.20	2.38	2.57	2.75	2.93	3.12
23	.96	1.15	1.34	1.53	1.73	1.92	2.11	2.30	2.49	2.68	2.88	3.07	3.26
24	1.00	1.20	1.40	1.60	1.80	2.00	2.20	2.40	2.60	2.80	3.00	3.20	3.40
25	1.04	1.25	1.46	1.67	1.88	2.08	2.29	2.50	2.71	2.72	3.13	3.33	3.54
26	1.08	1.30	1.52	1.73	1.95	2.17	2.38	2.60	2.82	3.03	3.25	3.47	3.68
27	1.13	1.35	1.58	1.80	2.03	2.25	2.48	2.70	2.93	3.15	3.38	3.60	3.83
28	1.17	1.40	1.63	1.87	2.10	2.33	2.57	2.80	3.03	3.27	3.50	3.73	3.97
29	1.21	1.45	1.69	1.93	2.18	2.42	2.66	2.90	3.14	3.38	3.63	3.87	4.11
30	1.25	1.50	1.75	[illegible]	2.25	2.50	2.75	3.00	3.25	[illegible]	3.75	4.00	[illegible]

At the beginning of each fiscal year:

1. Find the average number of hours per year that each machine is used for five years running.
2. Multiply the dollar value of the machine by the average number of hours to get "dollar hours" of each machine.
3. Add all "dollar hours" to get total sum for each year (A).
4. Sum up total expenses during fiscal year just ended (D).
5. Divide D/A = E, to find the cost of the machines.
6. Multiply the value of each machine by E and that is the "cost" or "wages" of each machine per hour.[12]

Taylor's criticism of this method was that exact "costs" for each machine would hold true only if expenses or work hours per machine varied from previous years. Taylor explained his system as follows:

> I apportion at the end of a period the actual expenses for that period, while Sellers attempts at the beginning of each year to forsee two of the important and necessarily variable and undeterminable conditions for the coming year and then charges his cost in proportion to these assumed conditions whether they are realized or not in actual practice.[13]

A more concise explanation of Taylor's cost system is found in "System of Bookkeeping and Returns as Introduced."[14] Barth comments that although this writeup was found in one of the Midvale record books, "it is absolutely certain that he had not while still with that company developed the style of bookkeeping therein briefly

---

[12]Adapted from F.W. Taylor, "Description of Sellers Method of Determining Costs," (unpublished, F.W. Taylor Collection, Stevens Institute of Technology, Hoboken, New Jersey), p. 1.

[13]Ibid., p. 2.

[14]F.W. Taylor, "System of Bookkeeping and Returns as Introduced," Germantown, Philadelphia, no date (unpublished, F.W. Taylor Collection, Stevens Institute of Technology, Hoboken, New Jersey).

outlined."[15] In this document which is primarily related to bookkeeping Taylor makes some reference to a cost system. He relates:

> A detailed cost sheet showing the cost of every article manufactured during the month and a comparison of this cost with its cost the last time the article was manufactured. This is the best check that I know regarding the efficiency of superintendents and foremen.[16]

As we proceed through the cases in this chapter, Taylor's sophistication in accounting can be seen to develop and his dependence on some form of standard costing is evident. Midvale Steel was only a start, but the rate table for example, was one place where the time motion studies produced cost information that could be used in accurately predetermining the labor cost of production.

The Manufacturing Investment Company

The Manufacturing Investment Company was a paper manufacturer with mills in Madison, Maine and Appleton, Wisconsin. The process of converting wood into paper, required the wood, along with sulphurous acid, to be placed in a steel tank (a digestor) and cooked for some forty hours until only pulp remained. Taylor's job as manager of the Madison Mill included the designing of

---

[15]Barth, "Eight Large Gray Canvas Covered Books," p. 5.

[16]Taylor, "System of Bookkeeping and Returns as Introduced," p. 1.

equipment, constructing the remainder of the Mill, and producing paper at the lowest possible cost.

After resigning from Midvale, Taylor served as the general manager of Manufacturing Investment (1890-1893). It was during this period that "he was forced by the requirements of this position to give heed to the details of accounting."[17] His position as manager enabled Taylor to be more independent of his superiors, but he also had more responsibilities than previously. It was at Manufacturing Investment that Taylor set seriously to study general bookkeeping and accounting, and to this end got in touch with William D. Basley, an expert railroad accountant of the times. It was by certain modifications of Basley's accounting methods to suit manufacturing plants, that Taylor developed what is described as "Taylor's Interlocking Cost and Accounting System."[18]

The cost accounting system developed at Manufacturing Investment is but another example of the total scope of the Taylor system. The Taylor system affected every part of the work process, with the cost department exerting the control element necessary for maintaining the standards. By comparison of the estimated and actual costs, the cost department was able to control the

---

[17]Copley, Frederick W. Taylor, Vol. I, p. 363.

[18]Barth, "Eight Large Gray Canvas Covered Books," p. 6.

quality and rate of production. Thus, though the accounting system developed at Manufacturing Investment was not completely refined, Taylor's total system was substantially improved by this introduction to the details of accounting.

The Bethlehem Steel Company

The Bethlehem Steel Company, a subsidiary of Bethlehem Steel Corporation was located in South Bethlehem, Pennsylvania. Begun in 1860 by Augustus and Frances Wolle as Bethlehem Iron Company, the name was changed in 1899. Though primarily manufacturing steel forgings for industry, in the 1890's it expanded its markets to include government contract work. With this new government work, Bethlehem Steel Company, employing between five thousand and six thousand men, found a need for new investments of capital and a more efficient works management system.

Taylor was attracted to Bethlehem, because he saw a golden opportunity of applying and instituting his concepts of work management. He negotiated for nearly a year with both R.P. Linderman, president of the Bethlehem Steel Company and Joseph Wharton, a financier and a major stockholder in the company, concerning the terms of employment. He began working there in May, 1898, after his "conditions of employment" were agreed upon by the Board of Directors. Taylor felt that if his system was to be fully operative and successful, he would need full authority to fire people disloyal to his system. (This apparently was a protective measure learned from his experience at Midvale, where the workers vehemently opposed the piece work and elementary time study systems) His salary demands were $35.00 per day, plus $5.00 per day for expenses,[19] an exceptionally high salary for the times.

Taylor began his work on May 27, 1898, and the first of his series of recommendations was submitted the same day. The subject of the recommendation was the "desirability of establishing standards throughout the works." This recommendation called for the standardization of every detail of the business. This is important in that it was his first recommendation to the company and was of highest priority. Control through standardization was the means to the end of increased production and profit; the primary goal of Bethlehem Steel in the 1890's.

Bethlehem Steel Company was a testing and experimental stage for the application of Taylor's system. Certain phases of Taylor's system were not implemented due to disagreements between Taylor and the management of the company. Taylor, in a letter to President Linderman states that "I was employed by your Company some three years ago to introduce a new system of management, accounting, etc. into your works."[20] Linderman, on the other hand, thought

---

[19]Letter from F.W. Taylor to Robert Linderman, Boston, Mass., January 19, 1898.

[20]Letter from F.W. Taylor to R.P. Linderman, So. Bethlehem, Pennsylvania, April 4, 1901.

that Taylor had been employed to increase general production levels and to introduce the piece work wage system. Taylor considered his authority over matters pertaining to his system to be absolute; this created the friction that eventually led to his leaving Bethlehem in 1901. He wrote "I do not want any authority in any matters except those immediately affecting my system of management and accounting, but I respectfully request that the various Officers of the Company be instructed to carry out all orders which may be given them by me in relation to these subjects."[21] It is apparent from this passage that Taylor considered both accounting and management as important elements of his system. The two elements complemented each other, could not be separated, and were interdependent.

In Recommendation #7 of September 23, 1898, Taylor submitted a report outlining the cost and accounting system he proposed to install. Taylor prefaced his proposals by indicating that the method which he "believes to be the best is in general the modern railroad system of accounting adopted and modified to suit the manufacturing business."[22] The chief aim of such a system was to obtain the information required by internal management for cost control or financial statement preparation. The cost system Taylor

---

[21]Letter from F.W. Taylor to R.P. Linderman, So. Bethlehem, Pennsylvania, April 4, 1901.

[22]Letter from F.W. Taylor to R.P. Linderman, So. Bethlehem, Pennsylvania, September 23, 1898.

recommended "should insure an accurate determination of the cost of all goods manufactured . . . and include complete comparative cost statements."[23]

Included in the report was a statement that Taylor would guarantee his system's effectiveness and accuracy if:

1. The entire accounting system was given a fair trial of three months before changes were made.

2. The decision of Taylor's would be paramount in any dispute over details of the system.[24]

On August 2, 1899, Taylor related that such a dispute of authority occurred when Taylor directed an employee to rule up a "voucher" blank in preparation for an accounts payable system based on vouchers. The employee regarded this procedure as unnecessary and appealed directly to Linderman for intervention. Linderman decided with Taylor and against the other employee on August 1, 1899, "so that no work was done on book or cost keeping between May 15 and August 1st."[25] This was a test of Taylor's power to decide the course of the accounting system. This round was won by Taylor, but the disputes continued for the duration of his stay and eventually led to his dismissal by Linderman as of May 1, 1901.

---

[23] *Ibid.*

[24] *Ibid.*

[25] *Ibid.* This is a note written by Taylor on the bottom of his letter to Linderman.

In the last letter written by Taylor to Linderman before his dismissal, Taylor requested again that he be given "the authority to see that my directions are properly carried out and in harmony with the new system."[26] This lack of authority was the most pervasive problem that inhibited the complete introduction and acceptance of the Taylor system into Bethlehem Steel Company. This request was denied.

Although few accounting reports from Bethlehem Steel still exist, Taylor's views on scientific management and on the necessity for accurate cost information useful for decision-making are obvious. His statements demonstrate his view of the reliance of management on good cost information and he attempted to implement a complete system of management.

One of the accounting forms found among the documents in the F.W. Taylor Collection that pertains to Bethlehem is a "Sheet for Determining Relative Cost Numbers." This form was an early attempt at an accurate determination of the costs of production and all of the components thereof. On the form, the costs of different size planers that occupied varying amounts of floor space were determined with specific reference to depreciation use, light, heat, insurance, taxes, etc. Coefficients were established and the time factor introduced in order to develop a

---

[26]Letter from F.W. Taylor to R.P. Linderman, S. Bethlehem, Pennsylvania, April 4, 1901.

comparative cost basis for the use of different machines. This was a sophisticated accounting tool for determining the standard costs of different machines used in production. A copy of this form is included as Exhibit 5. Though the form did produce a breakdown of the costs of production and could be used for the determination of standards, the form was never used. Thus, though Taylor did make advances in his system while at Bethlehem Steel, no standard costing was performed there. This is primarily due to the problems that developed between Taylor and Linderman. This form, prepared many years before the accounts of scientific management and standard cost accounting appeared in the periodicals, demonstrates the use of the concepts in industry through Taylor's consulting engagements, before 1911.

After Taylor's stay at Bethlehem, he retired from active employment and worked only on a consulting basis. This proved to be a better means by which Taylor's system could be installed in a large number of companies. As a consultant, Taylor supervised the introduction of his system in several companies concurrently. Taylor became the spokesman and symbol for scientific management in use.

Eastern Manufacturing Company

Sanford E. Thompson, an associate of Taylor's, was instrumental in installing scientific management in the plants of the Eastern

EXHIBIT 5

DEPARTMENT DM BUILDING MACHINE NO. 2[27]

Relative Cost Number
Month Day Year

On Buildings

Old Shop Symbol	New Shop Symbol	Name of Machine	Size	Bed	Description	Relative Cost Number
43		Planer	20½"		Bement, Miles & Co. #663	1
107		"	20½"		Wm. Sellers & Co. #810	
116		"	20½"		Bement, Miles & Co. #725	

Floor Space Sq. Feet	Depreciation in Style	Insur-ance	Taxes	Stores and Repairs	Light	Heat	Water	Caring and Cleaning	Total
100									
150									
100									

[27]Sheet for determining Relative Cost Numbers, Bethlehem Steel Company File (F.W. Taylor Collection, Stevens Institute of Technology, Hoboken, New Jersey).

EXHIBIT 5 (continued)

On Machines

Cost	% per year	Depreciation in Style	Insurance	Taxes	Stores	Repairs	Tools and	Inspector, speed boss, foreman and clerical Mte.

Total Machine Items	Co-efficient	Relative Time	Factor Coefficient Time	Power (Steam)	POWER ON ENGINES, LINE			
					Depre-ciation in Style	Insur-ance	Taxes	Stores

SHARTING, ETC.				
Repairs	Labor	Total Power Items	TOTAL	REMARKS

Manufacturing Company in 1915. The Eastern Manufacturing Company, with plants in Bangor and Lincoln, Maine, was one of the largest domestic manufacturers of writing paper. The plant at Bangor also operated its own pulp mill, part of the pulp being used for the paper and part for sale. The Bangor Mill employed about 800 people.

In an article relating the effects of scientific management on the Eastern Manufacturing Company, Thompson and his associates wrote:

> The logical process in the development of scientific methods is to begin with the handling, classification, and storage of the raw material; next establish control of the manufacturing process, and finally establish by scientific investigation standards of material and standard practice for operating the plant. It is evident that there are two distinct features involved in this: first, the introduction of a system in management, and second, the establishment of the standards.[28]

To present day scholars and businessmen, the goals, methods and achievements of the scientific management method seem straightforward, logical and almost as if common sense were the only required tools for standardization. A look at the manner in which a business was run before scientific management and a comparison of the after effects of scientific management will give a clearer indication of the value of this standardization system. Before the adoption of the Taylor system, the Eastern Manufacturing Company

---

[28]Sanford E. Thompson, William O. Lichtner, Keppele Hall, and Henry J. Guild, "Development of Scientific Methods of Management in a Manufacturing Plant," Trans. ASME, Vol. XXXIX (1917), p. 127.

had each foreman controlling the work in his own department subject to minor changes by his superiors. Thus, the foreman assigned the shop orders and specified when and which materials, men and machines were to be used to complete the job. More often than not, the materials needed were not on hand, or there was a great backlog of orders so that the men had to be worked overtime:

> with the incident extra expense and dissatisfaction of all concerned. In the filling of orders there was the same old story of broken promises, notwithstanding the best efforts of the Sales Department and the Manufacturing Department.[29]

With the installation of the Taylor system, a Planning Department was created which controlled in detail the progress of every order through the mill. Thus, each man had specific job tasks, with only a few men responsible for the overall production process. The standardization and control mechanisms enabled the paper to be produced at a lower cost. Standard methods were developed "of taking time and in getting these methods so that the results of different operators would be comparable."[30]

In a Standing Order about the inspection of costs it is stated that the "Inspection of Cost applies to each and every

---

[29] *Ibid.*, p. 130.

[30] *Ibid.*, p. 172.

item that enters into the Mill Cost of Operating the Eastern Manufacturing Company."[31] A standard cost system is evident in this company's operations. With the time elements and quality of the product standardized and placed in a format so that the results would be comparable, the cost of production was also standardized. Thus, we find instructions for the cost of inspecting specific processes with regard to standard costs.

> The Bailers and Washers hours must be compared with [a] standard and [a] report made of extraordinary increases or decreases. [With] The final cost per cwt of dryed rags weighed into Bailers, . . . [a] report is made [that] should be [the] standard, but if different from the standard cost, why should be explained.[32]

Current operating expenses were compared with previous operating expenses in the operating Expense Ledger. A standard:

> cost of operating the various machines, with the exception of direct labor, should be very uniform. The direct labor increase or decreases will be explained by our monthly load factor report.[33]

It is apparent from this that standard costs had been developed for each operation in the production process. The role of the cost inspectors was to determine any discrepancies from the standards and then determine the reason that the cost was greater or less

---

[31] Eastern Manufacturing Company, Standing Order No. 26, August 30, 1915 (F.W. Taylor Collection, Stevens Institute of Technology, Hoboken, New Jersey), p. 1.

[32] *Ibid.*, p. 2.

[33] *Ibid.*, p. 3-4.

than the standard. The conclusion of the treatise requires the cost inspectors to "carefully compare all figures leaving the Cost Department with standards provided and note increases or decreases with satisfactory reasons."[34] This is further evidence that standard cost systems had been installed in organizations some time before they were written about in published articles.

The Link-Belt Company

In installing the Taylor system at Link-Belt, Carl G. Barth and Horace K. Hathaway did most of the work, with Taylor acting as the unpaid (because of his friendship with Barth and Hathaway) consultant and supervisor. Numerous articles were written about Link-Belt, and it must be regarded as one of the better examples of Taylor's complete system.

The Nicetown, Pennsylvania, plant of Link-Belt Company was the first installation of scientific management in its entirety made "after Mr. Taylor had carried out his development work at the plant of Bethlehem Steel Company."[35] The introduction of the Taylor System began in 1904 when Barth was employed to supervise and investigate the work process. The plant employed 325 men, and manufactured gears and wheels with semi-automatic machines.

---

[34]*Ibid.*, p. 4.

[35]L.P. Alford, "Scientific Management in Use," *American Machinist*, Vol. XXX, No. 14 (April, 1912), p. 548.

The first procedure of installation was the "accumulation and systematizing of data from which the equipment of the shop could be properly standardized and arranged."[36] The emphasis on standardization was paramount. Location of machinery, work processes equipment, and products were all standardized.

The introduction of time study created changes in the planning, routing and cost-keeping departments. Time study brought about standardized differential piece rates which enabled the management to determine their costs before production began. In its crude form, this was the basic structure of the standard cost system.

In referring to the entire scientific management process at Link-Belt, L.P. Alford stated: "The central idea in all this was to provide means whereby the work could be thoroughly thought out before it was presented to the shop for execution; and then provide the best possible shop conditions for its prosecution."[37]

It is clear from correspondence between Taylor and Richard Yerkes, Sales Manager of Link-Belt, that the comparison of estimated and actual costs was an integral part of the cost department's operations. Yerkes wrote to Taylor:

> We last Fall commenced using in our estimating department the cost factors and figures obtained from the Taylor

---

[36] Ibid., p. 548.

[37] Ibid.

> System records, and the writer has much pleasure in advising you that we have just completed the table of costs of all what we term 'engineering jobs' which show that our actual costs are 3/4 of 1% less than the estimated.[38]

Taylor replied to Yerkes' letter relating that "it is most gratifying to me to see how closely your estimates agree with the actual."[39]

Accompanying Yerkes' letter is a copy of the form used by the estimating department at Link-Belt. (See Exhibit 6) This is an important document that indicates the use of a standard cost system in the Link-Belt Company. Further, the letter of acknowledgement from Taylor indicates that there the estimates were akin, in every way, with predetermined cost standards as we know them today.

H.H. Franklin Company

The H.H. Franklin Company produced the Franklin Car at its plant in Syracuse, New York. The company was established in 1902 and produced one hundred cars per month. The business was quite sucessful until "the business slump of 1907, which was acutely felt

---

[38]Letter from Richard Yerkes to Frederick W. Taylor, Nicetown, Pennsylvania, May 27, 1908.

[39]Letter from F.W. Taylor to Richard Yerkes, Philadelphia, Pennsylvania, May 28, 1908.

EXHIBIT 6

ESTIMATED

NAME	ORDER NO.	SELL. COST MACHINERY	S. C. DWGS.	S. C. ERECTION	FREIGHT	COMM. ETC.
		129,738.51	13,799.15	3,797.83	4580.15	745.55

ACTUAL

SELL. COST MACHINERY	S. C. DWGS.	S. C. ERECTION	FREIGHT	COMM. ETC.	COMPLETE SELLING COST	SELL. PRICE
130,772.80	12,479.28	3,260.40	3,742.11	736.92	150,992.11	155,154.[illegible]

by the whole automobile industry."[40] The Franklin Company decided to investigate the Taylor system, due primarily to an enlightened management who perceived a very definite advantage from the adoption of this system into their company. The investigation of the Taylor system lasted four years, including several trips to the Tabor Manufacturing Company by managers of the Franklin Company to see first hand the Taylor system in operation. Continuous correspondence with Taylor and Barth established the changes in the Franklin Company that were necessary to comply with the strict specific specifications of the Taylor system.

Barth related to the management of the Franklin Company those principal things that needed to be done to establish the system:

1. The preparation and maintenance of each tool in the best possible condition.
2. The standardization of feeds and speeds on all similar machines.
3. The providing of tool rooms with equipment of tools and jigs.
4. The mechanical operation of all jobs.
5. The establishment of standards.
6. The settling of a definite operating time for each part made.[41]

The advantages of this system specifically related to established standards including increased quality and output, decreased costs and a definitive cost standard for each unit produced.

---

[40]George D. Babcock, The Taylor System in Franklin Management (New York: The Engineering Magazine Company, 1918).

[41]Ibid., p. 12.

Barth introduced the Taylor system in 1912, and the management was most receptive to the changes and positive effects of the process.

In establishing a standard equitable hourly rate of pay, several factors were considered that were intimately related to one another. The general equation for the basic rate, where the premium method of payment is used, as deduced by us is:

$$r = \left[\left(\frac{K(B \quad (1+1+m+ny) + R) \qquad (1 + 2e)}{V \ (1 + 1.3E - .3e) \ (1 + .35P_a + S}\right)\left(P_t + P_a \ (1 + .5e)\right)\right]C$$

and for the determination of labor and indirect cost (not including materials) is:

$$.X = (r \ (1 + i) + R) \ t$$

The definitions of terms follow. They are common in both equations:

r = Base hourly rate man is to receive

K = A constant, when V is 100 per cent, to bring worker under standard conditions to standard rate

B = Fundamental base rate, temporarily that of 1905

m = Percentage allowed for each extra process known or learned

i = Percentage of increase in living since 1905, taken on the 15th of January, April, July and October of each year

n = Percentage allowed for years of connected service

y = Years of such service

R = Fixed charges rate per hour which man has chance to modify

e = Percentage of premium earned on time allowance

V = 100, which is the standard accomplishment per cent

E = Standard permium task time set

P_a = Percentage of time absent or late

S = Value of spoiled work per producing hours worked

P_t = Percentage of time under task

P_d = Percentage of time spent on non-task or straight time work

C = Co-operation and conduct

X = Labor and fixed charge cost

t = Time taken to do the work[42]

This equation is the Standard Cost Formula for setting wage rates. One of the interesting elements in this formula is the Percentage of Increase in Living Costs which includes food, shelter, clothing and fuel, for comparison in future years with actual increases in living costs.

The Standard Premium Task Time (E) was one of the clearest examples of a standard cost employed in the cost system of this company. "This value is the percentage of premium which the worker should earn as against (e) the percentage of premium which he actually does earn."[43]

In performance appraisal and determining wage rate increases, standard costs were pervasively used. The appraisal of work performed

---

[42] *Ibid.*, pp. 84-85.

[43] *Ibid.*, p. 97.

using a comparison of "record" (actual) and standard is shown in the Workman's Rating Report forms shown in Exhibit 7.[44] Further, the comparison of previous performance with present performance is also made. This is another example of the sophistication involved in the use of standard costs in managerial decision-making.

Another document that also concerns wage rates, and standard costs is the Comparative Statement of Cost and Earnings shown in Exhibit 8.[45] This further illustrates the use of standard costs, through variances, in performance evaluation.

It is evident from the previous documents and forms that the standard cost system was an integral part of the Franklin adoption of scientific management for wage rates. As stated previously by Taylor, scientific management should be adaptable to the specific needs of the manufacturing concern, making sure only that it does not violate the essential principles of standardization, rate fixing, routing, and planning and control. The H.H. Franklin Company's use of standards in wage determinations is in keeping with the fundamental principles of Taylor's system and proved to be an advanced system of scientific management and standard cost accounting.

---

[44] Ibid., pp. 104-105.

[45] Ibid., p. 174.

EXHIBIT 7

H.H. FRANKLIN COMPANY

Workmen's Rating Report Forms

FORM A-1387 MFG.

WORKMAN'S RATING REPORT

NAME	CLOCK NO.	OLD RATE	NEW RATE
H.K.	532	.43	.495

NEW RATE BEGINS	MO. 7	DAY 1	YR. 16	CONTINUES UNTIL	MO. 10	DAY 1	YR. 16	REPORT ISSUED	6	30	16
PERIOD BEGINS	4	8	16	PERIOD ENDS	6	3	16	PERIOD LENGTH	450 Hrs.		

FACTOR	EXPLANATION	RECORD	STANDARD
e-E	Per cent of task time earned	42.7%	33.3%
Pa	" " " absence per hour worked	2.2%	0
Pd	" " " time spent on day work	31 %	10
Ps	" " " time suspended	0 %	0
S	Average cost of spoiled work per hour	$.00	0
M	No. of major processes can do	5¾	2
Y	Years of continuous service	10.4	5
C	Conduct and co-operation	100%	100%

REMARKS:

Your record through the current period will increase or decrease your rate for the coming period.

AUTHORIZED	APPROVED	APPROVED
E.B.D.	G.S.M.	J.
PRODUCTION MANAGER	SUPERINTENDENT	DEPT. FOREMAN

FORM A-1387 MFG.

12/5/16 **WORKMAN'S RATING REPORT**

NAME Crank Grd.	CLOCK NO.	OLD RATE	NEW RATE
Mr.K.	532	495	535

NEW RATE BEGINS	MO. 9	DAY 18	YR. 16	CONTINUES UNTIL	MO. 12	DAY 18	YR. 16	REPORT ISSUED	9	18	16
PERIOD BEGINS	6	3	16	PERIOD ENDS	8	26	16	PERIOD LENGTH	630 Hrs.		

FACTOR	EXPLANATION	RECORD	STANDARD
e-E	Per cent of task time earned	60%	33.3%
Pa	" " " absence per hour worked	1.4%	0 %
Pd	" " " time spent on day work	6 %	10 %
Ps	" " " time suspended	0 %	0 %
S	Average cost of spoiled work per hour	$.003	$.00
M	No. of major processes can do	5¾	2
Y	Years of continuous service	10.6	5
C	Conduct and co-operation	100%	100

REMARKS:

Your excellent record of premium earnings as well as low absence has put your rate up this additional amount.

Your record through the current period will increase or decrease your rate for the coming period. R.M.H.

AUTHORIZED	APPROVED	APPROVED
E.B.D.	G.S.M.	J.
PRODUCTION MANAGER	SUPERINTENDENT	DEPT. FOREMAN

EXHIBIT 8

H.H. FRANKLIN COMPANY

Comparative Statement of Cost and Earnings

H. K. ....No. 532 Dates Chosen	Before First Rating Apr. 21-2-3-4-5-6-7	Since Last Rating Sept. 19-20-1-3-25	Per Cent. Increase	 Decrease
Rate per hour = r.	$.355	$.535	50	..
Overhead per hr. = R.	.400	.510	27.5	..
Prem. time allowed per piece	104 min.	104 min.	0	0
Lot size	35 min.	35 min.	0	0
Time allowed, per lot	60.6 hrs.	60.6 hrs.	0	0
Time taken, per lot	35.6 hrs.	24.6 hrs.	..	30.9
Time saved, per lot	25.0 hrs.	36.0 hrs.	44	..
Prem. hrs. earned, per lot	12.5 hrs.	18.0 hrs.	44	..
Per Cent. of Prem. hr. earned per lot = e	35 1–10%	73 2–10%	108.6	..
Time taken per crank = t	1.017 hrs.	.7029 hrs.	..	30.9
Cost per crank X = [r(1+e)+R]t } =	[0.355 (1.351)+0.51] 1.017 $1.0064	[0.535 (1.732)+0.51] 0.7029 $1.0097	.. 0.31	.. ..
Weekly Earnings Std.	$23.36	$44.38	90	..

Case Summary

Taylor's intense interest in accounting led him to write a long treatise, "Cost Keeping Under the Taylor System of Shop Management." This is a detailed description of the theoretical issues involved in his system and the manner in which the practical goals of standardization in cost analysis can be achieved. Although no date can be determined as the date of writing, it is evident that it was during or after his experience at Tabor Manufacturing.

In the section dealing with the Expense Distribution Sheet, Taylor explained what he meant by an estimate:

> The relative cost number of a machine is a factor computed for the use of distributing Shop Expense. It is obtained by estimating the manufacturing cost under ideal conditions for a certain period, usually a year.[46]

This is the essence of the standard cost system. Thus, his use of the word "estimate" can be equated with the "standard cost" definition in Chapter I of this thesis.

Though other examples of scientific management installations could be cited to show similar systems, it is felt that the previous case studies are a representative selection of cases that indicate the impact of scientific management on the development of the standard cost system in industry. The Taylor system always stressed

---

[46] Cost Keeping Under the Taylor System of Shop Management (unpublished, F.W. Taylor Collection, Stevens Institute of Technology, Hoboken, New Jersey), p. 29.

the accurate predetermination of performance standards and the comparison of those standards with actual performance. Thus, the standard cost per unit was compared with the actual cost per unit. This impact of scientific management on the development of the standard cost system was clearly seen in the cases presented in this chapter to have occurred in Taylor's consulting years before the articles published in the journals discussed this advance.

CHAPTER VII

SUMMARY

Importance of Study

In previous historical works on the development of managerial accounting, credit has been given to the scientific management school for its impact on the development of the standard cost system. But, no one has yet clearly demonstrated this relationship. The American Accounting Association's Committee on Accounting History suggested as a needed research topic, the "effects of the 'scientific management' movement on the evolution of standard cost accounting."[1] The most important work in the area of managerial accounting history done by Garner, Parker, and Solomons also indicated the need for this research.

This study was undertaken in order to provide for accountants—academic and otherwise—a clear exposition of the importance of the scientific management movement on the historical development of managerial accounting, with special reference to the standard cost system. This thesis demonstrated two important points:

---

[1]American Accounting Association, Report of the Committee on Accounting History, Accounting Review, Supplement to Volume XLV, 1970, p. 53.

1. The scientific management movement had an important and direct effect on the development of the standard cost system.

2. This effect was due to the requirements of scientific management in its application in industry.

Chapter V of this thesis traced, through a discussion of the literature of the times, the development of standard cost concepts in accounting. With the exception of the contributions made by Harrington Emerson beginning in 1908, the development of standard costs generally accompanied the popularization of scientific management in the literature following the Eastern Rate Case hearings of 1910 and 1911. Emerson's later work[2] demonstrated the relationship between actual and standard costs. His standard cost formula showed the sophistication in Emerson's thinking, and also appears to be the first application of the concept of variances. Solomons suggests, and it is borne out by the literature, that from 1912 on there was a change in emphasis from "the ascertainment of what it costs to carry out an industrial process or function."[3] Such notables as Harrison, Bunnell, and Scovell made their contributions

---

[2]Harrington Emerson, Twelve Principles of Efficiency (New York: John R. Dunlap, 1911) and Efficiency as a Basis for Operation and Wages (New York: Engineering Magazine Company, 1912).

[3]David Solomons, "The Historical Development of Costing," in David Solomons, ed. Studies in Cost Analysis (Homewood, Illinois: Richard D. Irwin, 1968), p. 46.

to the development of the standard cost system, after 1911. Thus, the discussion of the literature clearly showed the impact of scientific management on the development of the standard cost system.

In Chapter VI, case studies were used to illustrate the use of standard cost concepts in companies that implemented the Taylor system of scientific management. It was clearly shown that the standard costing systems were in existence in industry before their discussion in the literature. It was further shown that the development of standard costing was a logical outgrowth of scientific management because of the need of scientific management for standard cost information.

One of the goals of scientific management was to increase efficiency and productivity through a pre-determination of the rate of work (through the use of elementary time studies). Standard time periods for a given operation required standard tools and equipment for the work to be done. This required standard methods of routing the work, standard methods of operating procedures, and standard determinations of product costs or standard costs. Standardization in all phases of the production process was a fundamental principle of Taylor's scientific management system. Standardization was necessary so that a comparison between actual performance could be made. The difference between these two levels of performance, the variance, was necessary for the exercise of management control and overall efficiency of operations.

Thus, with the utilization of these two research methods--the extensive discussion of the literature and the case studies--this study has been able to demonstrate that scientific management had an important and direct effect on the standard cost system. This study has attempted to demonstrate that scientific management preceeded the development of standard cost accounting. It has attempted to demonstrate through both the literature and the cases that a time lag existed. In summary, this time lag can best be seen in Exhibit 9.

The time lag between the development of scientific management and the development of standard costing is shown in this exhibit. It demonstrates that scientific management preceeded the development of the standard cost system. For example, the wage plans proposed in the 1880's which became an important basis for scientific management, demanded standard costing methods. These standard cost methods began to appear at the beginning of the 1900's. But, it was not until 1908-1912 that standard cost systems began to appear.

This study has shown that standard cost accounting was an important element of the scientific management system; that scientific management in its application in industry needed standard cost

EXHIBIT 9

THE DEVELOPMENT OF SCIENTIFIC MANAGEMENT AND THE STANDARD COST SYSTEM

Scientific Management		Cost Accounting
	1880	
1882-Henry Towne-"Shop System of the Yale Lock Manufacturing Company" an account of a successful shop system installed.		
	1885	1885-Captain Henry Metcalf-*Cost of Manufactures*, well known work concerned with determination of actual costs.
1886-Midvale Steel Company-wage rate tables for determining standard wage costs.		1887-Garcke & Fells-*Factory Accounts*, early English application of overhead and actual cost determination.
	1890	
1893-F.W. Taylor-*Bookkeeping Under the Taylor System*. First attempt of Taylor at record-keeping.		
1895-F.W. Taylor-"A Piece Rate System." First article on Taylor System proposed elementary time-study and differential rate.	1895	1896-H.M. Lane-"A Method of Determining Selling Price," introduced a cost sheet comparing actual and estimated costs.
1896-F.W. Taylor-"Cost-Keeping Under the Taylor System," an attempt at developing a technique for cost-keeping.		

EXHIBIT 9 (Continued)

1898-Bethlehem Steel Company-Standardization and Control Recommendation #7. Report outlines Taylor's cost and accounting system.

1900

1901-Alexander H. Church-"The Proper Distribution of Establishment Charges," discusses relationship between control and comparison of standards with actual costs.

1902-Percy Longmuir-"Recording and Interpreting Foundry Costs," suggests the measurement of actual costs with standards based on experience rather than time study.

1903-F.W. Taylor-Shop Management, introduces standardization concept for all phases of operations.

1904-Link Belt Company installs Taylor System.

1905

1906-D.C. Eggleston-"Factory Cost Accounting." Standard costs used for comparison of production costs. No definition of standard.

1908-John Whitmore-"Shoe Factory Cost Accounts." Discussion of what standard costing should be.

1908-Harrington Emerson-"Efficiency as a Basis for Operation." "Comparison of costs" statement developed. Based on actual vs. realizable standard amounts.

EXHIBIT 9 (Continued)

1910

1910-F.W. Taylor-Principles of Scientific Management published elaboration of Taylor's system.

1910-Beginning of Eastern Rate Case hearings. Scientific management proponents testified, which led to popularization of scientific management.

1911-Harrington Emerson-Twelve Principles of Efficiency. Presents sophisticated standard cost formula, including variances

1912-Congressional Hearings on Taylor System.

1912-H.H. Franklin Company-Standard Cost Formula, and comparative statement of Cost and Earnings used.

1912-Sterling Bunnell-"Are Profits a Proper Measure of Efficiency," discusses uses of standard costs for internal control.

1913-C.A. Harrington-"The Relation of Detailed Planning and the Cost of Production," explains the need for using standard cost techniques in scientific management systems.

EXHIBIT 9 (Continued)

1915-Eastern Manufacturing Company-Standing Order No. 26. Time elements and product costs standardized.

1915

1916-H.L. Gantt-"Production and Sales." Leading exponent of scientific management sees need for standard costs in production process.

1919-G. Charter Harrison-"The Scientific Basis of Cost Accounting." Sophisticated use of cost variances.

1921-G. Charter Harrison-Cost Accounting to Aid Production. Complete standard cost system, including analysis of cost variances.

information. Thus, the standard costing system would not have developed had standard cost information not been required for the successful implementation of scientific management. Further then, no plausible alternatives are seen to exist nor were other channels in existence at this period in history for the development of the standard cost system.

In the extensive literature search and in the extensive examination of company records, there was no evidence that a plausible alternative hypothesis exists. Further, there was no evidence that use of standard costing existed in businesses not touched by the scientific management school or the "efficiency" school. All relevant cases found were discussed in Chapter VI and none indicated significant advances to standard cost accounting by any authors or consultants other than those connected with "efficiency" or scientific management.

Research Methodology

The philosophical base at which the historian begins his research is important in that it affects the results and validity of the research process. The historical theory employed in this thesis is that the historian's role is one of interpretation of the facts, due to his inability to observe the events. The scientist, as opposed to the historian, gains his knowledge from the observation and experimentation of the events. The historian must seek out all known facts relevant to the event, and base his interpretation on this knowledge. Using this kind of theoretical base, we can conclude that history "is a continuous process of interaction between the historian and his facts, an unending dialogue between the present and the past."[4]

The effect of the theoretical base employed in this thesis is that all data relevant to the topic was sought out in order to "interpret" those events as they occurred. An extensive literature search was conducted that gathered all data, known to the author, concerning the subject at hand.

Managerial accountants have never had a study which conclusively demonstrated and traced the development of this field. Further, since the standard cost system is such an integral part of managerial accounting, as it is known today, its origin is enlightening to accountants generally and managerial accountants specifically. This study provides managerial accountants with new insight into their discipline. Further, as stated in Chapter I, only with studies of this kind can accounting continue to develop academically.

Finally, it is hoped that further research will be conducted on accounting history generally. Chapter I attempted to show the

---

[4]Edward H. Carr, What is History? (New York: Alfred A. Knopf, 1962), p. 35.

need in accounting for further research on its development. Hopefully, this study will spark new interests and new insights into accounting history.

APPENDIX A

A SELECTED LIST OF BUSINESSES THAT INSTALLED SCIENTIFIC MANAGEMENT

(Adapted from Elizabeth Gardner Hayward, A Classified Guide to the Frederick Winslow Taylor Collection, New York: American Society of Mechanical Engineers, 1951), pp. 31-33.

Acme Wire Co.
New Haven, Conn.

Bethlehem Steel Co.
Bethlehem, Penn.

Clothcraft Shops of the
Joseph & Feiss Co.
Cleveland, Ohio

Corona Typewriter Co., Inc.
Groton, New York

Cramp (The William) & Sons
Ship & Engine Building Co.
Philadelphia, Penn.

Dodge and Day
Philadelphia, Penn.

Eastern Manufacturing Co.
Bangor, Maine

Farrell Foundry and Machine Co.
Ansonia, Conn.

Forbes Lithograph Manufacturing
Chelsea, Mass.

Franklin (H.H.) Manufacturing Co.
Syracuse, New York

Goldie & McCullough
Gault, Ontario, Canada

Jones & Laughlin Steel Corp.
Pittsburgh, Penn.

Link-Belt Co.
Philadelphia, Penn.

Manufacturing Investment Co.
Madison, Maine

Midvale Steel Co.
Philadelphia, Penn.

Myers (Elwood) Co.

New England Butt Co.
Providence, Rhode Island

Northern Electrical Mfg. Co.
Madison, Wisconsin

Passaic Metal Ware Co.
Passaic, New Jersey

Penn Central Light & Power Co.

Pennsylvania Railroad Co.
Philadelphia, Penn.

Plimpton Press
Norwood, Mass.

Plymouth Cordage Co.
Plymouth, Mass.

APPENDIX A continued

Pullman Co.
Chicago, Ill.

Robins Conveying Belt Co.
New York, N.Y.

Sayles Bleacheries
Saylesville, Rhode Island

Sellers (William) & Co.
Philadelphia, Penn.

Simonds Rolling-Machine Co.
Fitchburg, Mass.

Smith & Furbush Machine Co.
Philadelphia, Penn.

Steel Motor Co. and the
Lorain Steel Co.
Johnstown, Penn.

Tabor Manufacturing Co.
Philadelphia, Penn.

Union Typewriter Co.
New York, N.Y.

Walworth Manufacturing Co.
South Boston, Mass.

Watertown Arsenal
Watertown, Mass.

Williams and Wilkins Co.
Boston, Mass.

Yale and Towne Manufacturing Co.
Stamford, Conn.

Bethlehem Steel Corporation

BETHLEHEM, PA 18016

September 23, 1971

IN REPLY REFER TO

BFB-90-A

Mr. Marc J. Epstein
College of Commerce
University of Saskatchewan
Saskatoon, Canada

Dear Mr. Epstein:

In the early 1950's, Bethlehem Steel organized a records planning division within its accounting department for the sole purpose of effecting more efficient as well as economical results in areas having to do with paperwork management. At that time, most records dating back as much as forty years were destroyed and any retained items dating back to the turn of the century are very few.

For this reason, it is not possible for us to contribute to your research having to do with the Taylor System and its relationship to the "Effects of Scientific Management in the Development of Standard Cost Accounting".

Very truly yours,

W. V. C. Setterley

Assistant Comptroller

FMC CORPORATION

MACHINERY GROUP HEADQUARTERS

PRUDENTIAL PLAZA, CHICAGO, ILLINOIS 60601 • TELEPHONE: (312) 346-1800

October 12, 1971

Mr. Marc J. Epstein
University of Saskatchewan
College of Commerce
Saskatoon, Canada

Dear Mr. Epstein:

I would like to thank you for your interest in the Link-Belt Corporation for your study of the "Effects of Scientific Management on the Development of Standard Cost Accounting". To bring you up to date, the Link-Belt Corporation was merged into the Machinery Group of the FMC Corporation in 1967. Unfortunately, because of the span of years since the period of time your study covers and the change in personnel over the years I have been unsuccessful in trying to locate any of the material or anyone familiar with the material you requested in your letter.

I am sorry we are unable to assist you, but I would like to thank you again for your interest in the Link-Belt organization.

Regards,

Edward H. Thorholm

EHT:np

Edward H. Thorholm
Cost Accounting Co-ordinator

THE ATCHISON, TOPEKA AND SANTA FE RAILWAY COMPANY

80 EAST JACKSON BOULEVARD, CHICAGO, ILLINOIS 60604

W. E. WILLINGHAM
VICE PRESIDENT AND
GENERAL AUDITOR

October 19, 1971

Mr. Marc J. Epstein
Assistant Professor of Accounting
College of Commerce
University of Saskatchewan
Saskatoon, Canada

Dear Mr. Epstein:

I have your letter of October 8 concerning your study of the "Effects of Scientific Management on the Development of Standard Cost Accounting".

I too, have heard that the Santa Fe Railway Company adopted some features of the Taylor System in its shops. To the best of my knowledge however there was no carryover into a cost accounting system. As you may well surmise no one presently connected with the Company has first hand knowledge of the installation and the effects on our cost accounting.

I would judge that adoption of the Taylor System to whatever extent it may have been used was applied strictly from an engineering management standpoint. In fact we are just now in the process of installing formal cost accounting in our system shops and from information obtained with that effort I would suspect very little, if any, effect of the Taylor System is still continuing.

In view of the foregoing, I do not believe we would be of much assistance in your study but extend my best wishes for its successful conclusion.

Yours truly,

W E Willingham

BIBLIOGRAPHY

Books

Addams, Jane. Twenty Years at Hull House. New York: The MacMillan Company, 1910. in The Progressives. Edited by Carl Resek. New York: Bobbs Merrill Company, Inc., 1967.

Aitken, Hugh. Taylorism at Watertown Arsenal: Scientific Management in Action 1908-1915. Cambridge: Harvard University Press, 1960.

The Annals Index from 1890-1935. Philadelphia: The American Academy of Political and Social Science, 1916.

Anyon, James T. Recollections of the Early Days of American Accountancy. New York: private printing, 1925.

Arnold, Horace Lucian. The Complete Cost Keeper. New York: Engineering Magazine Company, 1900.

________. The Factory Manager and Accountant: Some Examples of the Latest American Factory Practise. New York: Engineering Magazine Company, 1903.

Babcock, George D., Lieut. Col. The Taylor System in Franklin Management. New York: The Engineering Magazine Company, 1918.

Baltes, Frank William. The Cost of Printing. Portland, Oregon: Baltes, 1894.

Baugh, Frederick Henry. Principles and Practice of Cost Accounting for Accountants, Manufacturers, Mechanical Engineers, Teachers, & Students. Baltimore: F.H. Baugh, 1916.

Baughman, James P., ed. The History of American Management. Englewood Cliffs, New Jersey: Prentice-Hall, Inc., 1969.

Bean, Burt Clifford. The Cost of Production: The Principles of the Science of Costs. Chicago: System Company, 1905.

Bentley, Harry C. The Science of Accounts. New York: Ronald Press, 1913.

Book-Keeper Publishing Company, Ltd. Factory Cost Accounting. Detroit: Book-Keeper Publishing Company, 1900.

Boyd, J.H.H. Costing in Relation to Scientific Management. London: Industrial Reconstruction Council, 1919.

Brown, R. Gene, and Johnston, Kenneth S. Paciolo on Accounting. New York: McGraw-Hill Book Company, Inc., 1963.

Brown, Richard. A History of Accounting and Accountants. New York: Augustus M. Kelley, 1905.

Brummet, R. Lee. Overhead Costing: The Costing of Manufactured Products. Ann Arbor, Michigan: Bureau of Business Research, School of Business Administration, University of Michigan, 1957.

Carey, John L. The Rise of the Accounting Profession--From Technical to Professional 1896-1936. New York: American Institute of Certified Public Accountants, Inc., 1969.

Carr, Edward Hallett. What is History? New York: Alfred A. Knopf, 1961.

Chamberlain, John. Farewell to Reform: The Rise, Life, and Decay of the Progressive Mind in America. New York: John Day Company, 1932.

Chandler, Alfred D.; Bruchey, Stuart; and Galambos, Louis, eds. The Changing Economic Order: Readings in American Business and Economic History. New York: Harcourt, Brace & World, Inc., 1968.

________, and Salsbury, Stephen, eds. "The Railroads: Innovators in Modern Business Administration" in The Changing Economic Order. Edited by Chandler, Alfred D., Jr.; Bruchey, Stuart; and Galambos, Louis. New York: Harcourt, Brace & World, Inc., 1968.

Chellew, Henry. Human and Industrial Efficiency. New York: G.P. Putnam's Sons, 1920.

Church, Alexander Hamilton. Manufacturing Costs and Accounts. New York: McGraw-Hill Book Company, Inc., 1917.

________. Production Factors in Cost Accounting and Works Management. New York: Engineering Magazine Company, 1910.

Clark, J. Maurice. Studies in the Economics of Overhead Costs. Chicago: The University of Chicago Press, 1923.

Cole, William Morse. Cost Accounting for Institutions. New York: The Ronald Press Company, 1913.

Collingwood, R.G. The Idea of History. New York: Oxford University Press, 1946.

Cook, Charles Bannister. Factory Management. Detroit: Book-Keeper Publishing Company, 1906.

Copley, Frank Barkley. Frederick W. Taylor: Father of Scientific Management. New York: Harper and Brothers, 1923.

Crooks, James B. Politics & Progress: The Rise of Urban Progressivism in Baltimore, 1895-1911. Baton Rouge: Louisiana State University Press, 1968.

Drury, Horace B. Scientific Management: A History & Criticism. New York: author published, 1915.

East, John. Council Manager Government: The Political Thought of its Founder, Richard S. Childs. Chapel Hill: University of North Carolina Press, 1965.

Elbourne, Edward T. Costing Problem. London: Liberty Press, 1919.

Elton, G.R. The Practice of History. Sydney: Sydney University Press, 1967.

Ely, Richard T. Studies in the Evolution of Industrial Society. New York: The Macmillan Press, 1903.

Emerson, Harrington. Efficiency as a Basis for Operation & Wages. New York: Engineering Magazine Company, 1914.

________. The Twelve Principles of Efficiency. New York: Engineering Magazine Company, 1917.

Fink, Albert. Cost of Railroad Transportation, Railroad Accounts, and Governmental Regulation of Railroad Tariffs. Louisville, Kentucky: J.P. Morton & Company, 1875.

Freedman, Robert, ed. Marx on Economics. New York: Harcourt, Brace & World, Inc., 1961.

Garcke, Emile, and Fells, J.M. Factory Accounts: Their Principle and Practice. London: Crosby, Lockwood and Sons, 1887.

Garner, S. Paul. Evolution of Cost Accounting to 1925. Montgomery, Alabama: University of Alabama Press, 1954.

________. "Highlights in the Development of Cost Accounting" in Readings in Cost Accounting Budgeting and Control. Edited by William E. Thomas. Cincinnati: South-Western Publishing Company, 1955.

Garrison, E.E. Accounting Every Business Man Should Know. New York: Doubleday, Page & Company, 1910.

George, Claude S., Jr. The History of Management Thought. Englewood Cliffs, New Jersey: Prentice-Hall, Inc., 1968.

________. Management in Industry. Englewood Cliffs, New Jersey: Prentice-Hall, Inc., 1959.

Gilbreth, Frank. Primer of Scientific Management. New York: Van Nostrand Company, 1914.

Gillespie, Cecil. Standard & Direct Costing. Englewood Cliffs, New Jersey: Prentice-Hall, Inc., 1962.

Gillette, Halbert P., and Dana, Richard T. Cost Keeping and Management Engineering. New York and Chicago: The Myron C. Clark Publishing Company, 1909.

Goodyear, Samuel Horatio, and Goodyear, Lloyd E. Higher Accounting. Cedar Rapids: Goodyear-Marshall Publishing Company.

Gras, N.S.B., and Larson, Henrietta M. Casebook in American Business History. New York: Appleton-Century-Crofts, Inc., 1939.

Green, Wilmer. History and Survey of Accountancy. Brooklyn: Standard Text Press, 1930.

Haber, Samuel. Efficiency and Uplift. Chicago: The University of Chicago Press, 1964.

Hall, Harry Lovinas Celphas. Manufacturing Cost. Detroit: Book-Keeper Publishing Company, 1904.

Handlin, Oscar. The History of the United States, Vol. II. New York: Holt, Rinehart & Winston, 1968.

Harrison, G. Charter. Cost Accounting to Aid Production. New York: Engineering Magazine Company, 1921.

Hathaway, Charles E., and Griffith, James Bray. Factory Accounts: A Working Handbook of Departmental Organization and Methods as Applied to Factories. Chicago: American School of Correspondence, 1910.

Hawkins, L. Whittem. Cost Accounts: An Explanation of Principles and a Guide to Practice. London: Gee & Company, 1912.

Haynes, W. Warren, and Massey, Joseph L. Management Analysis, Concepts and Cases. Englewood Cliffs, New Jersey: Prentice-Hall, Inc., 1961.

Hayward, Elizabeth Gardner. A Classified Guide to the Frederick Winslow Taylor Collection. New York: American Society of Mechanical Engineers, 1951.

Hendricksen, Eldon S. Accounting Theory. Homewood, Illinois: Richard D. Irwin, Inc., 1965.

Hofstadter, Richard. The Age of Reform: from Bryan to FDR. New York: Knopf, 1955.

________, ed. The Progressive Movement 1900-1915. Englewood Cliffs, New Jersey: Prentice-Hall, Inc., 1963.

Horngren, Charles T. Cost Accounting: A Managerial Emphasis. Englewood Cliffs, New Jersey: Prentice-Hall, Inc., 1967.

Hoxie, Robert Franklin. Scientific Management and Labor. New York: Augustus M. Kelley, 1966.

Hughes. H. Stuart. History as Art and as Science. New York: Harper and Row, 1964.

Jackson, J. Hugh. "A Half-Century of Cost Accounting Progress" in Readings in Cost Accounting Budgeting and Control. Edited by William E. Thomas. Cincinnati: South-Western Publishing Company, 1955.

Johnson, Emory R. American Academy of Political and Social Science--Annals. Philadelphia: American Academy of Political and Social Science, 1903.

Kakar, Sudhir. Frederick Taylor: A Study in Personality and Innovation. Cambridge: The M.I.T. Press, 1970.

Kemp, William S. Departmental and Standard Costs. New York: National Association of Cost Accountants, 1923.

Kent, William. Bookkeeping and Cost Accounting for Factories. New York: John Wiley & Sons, Inc., 1918.

________. Investigating an Industry. New York: John Wiley & Sons, Inc., 1913.

Leffingwell, W.H. Scientific Office Management. Chicago. A.W. Shaw Company, 1917.

Lilley, Samuel. Men, Machines and History. New York: International Publishers, 1965.

Littleton, A.C. Accounting Evolution to 1900. New York: American Institute Publishing Company, 1933.

________, and Yamey. B.S. Studies in the History of Accounting. London: Sweet & Maxwell, Ltd., 1956.

Livesey, F.J. Laundry Accounts. London: Gee & Company, 1905.

Marple, Raymond P. National Association of Accountants on Direct Costing: Selected Papers. New York: The Ronald Press Company, 1965.

Marx, Karl. The Communist Manifesto. Chicago: Henry Regnery Company, 1954.

Merton, Robert K. "Latent Functions of the Machine" in American Urban History. Edited by Alexander B. Callow, Jr. New York: Oxford University Press, 1969.

Metcalfe, Henry. The Cost of Manufactures and the Administration of Workshops Public and Private. New York: Wiley, 1885.

Miller, Delbert C., and Form, William H. Industrial Sociology. New York: Harper and Brothers, 1951.

Mitchell, George A. Single Cost Accounts. London: Gee & Company, 1907.

Morrison, Samuel Eliot; Commager, Henry Steele; and Leuchtenberg, William E. The Growth of the American Republic, Vol. II. New York: Oxford University Press, 1969.

Moxey, Edward P. Principles of Factory Cost Keeping. New York: The Ronald Press Company, 1919.

Nichols, William G. Cost Finding. Chicago: American School of Correspondence, 1909.

________. Methods of Cost Finding in Cotton Mills. Waltham, Mass.: E.L. Barry, 1900.

Nicholson, Jerome Lee. Cost Accounting: Theory and Practice. New York: The Ronald Press Company, 1917.

________. Nicholson on Factory Organization and Costs. New York: Kohl Technical Publishing Company, 1909.

North, Douglass C. Growth and Welfare in the American Past. Englewood Cliffs, New Jersey: Prentice-Hall, Inc., 1966.

Parker, R.H. Management Accounting: an Historical Perspective. London: MacMillan and Company, Ltd., 1969.

Renier, G.J. History: It's Purpose and Method. New York: Harper & Row Publishers, 1950.

Resek, Carl, ed. The Progressives. New York: The Bobbs Merrill Company, Inc., 1967.

Roll, Sir Eric. An Early Experiment in Industrial Organisation. London: Frank Cass and Company, Ltd., 1930.

Ross, Edward A. The Old World in the New. New York, 1914.

Solomons, David. "The Historical Development of Costing" in Studies in Cost Analysis. Edited by David Solomons. Homewood, Illinois: Richard D. Irwin, Inc., 1968, Second Edition.

Spriegel, William R., and Myers, Clark E. The Writings of the Gilbreths. Homewood, Illinois: Richard D. Irwin, Inc., 1953.

Stacey, Nicholas A.H. English Accountancy--A Study in Social and Economic History 1800-1954. London: Gee & Company, Ltd., 1954.

Steffens, Lincoln. The Shame of the Cities. New York: Harper and Brothers, 1919.

Taylor, Frederick W. The Principles of Scientific Management. New York: Harper and Brothers, 1919.

________. Scientific Management. New York: Harper and Brothers, 1911.

________. Shop Management. New York: Harper and Brothers, 1911.

Thompson, C. Bertrand. How to Find Factory Costs. Chicago: A.W. Shaw Company, 1916.

________, ed. Scientific Management: A Collection of the more Significant Articles Describing the Taylor System of Management. Cambridge: Harvard University Press, 1914.

________. The Theory and Practice of Scientific Management. Boston: Houghton Mifflin, 1917.

Toynbee, Arnold J. A Study of History. (Abridgement of Volumes VII-X by D.C. Somervell). New York: Oxford University Press, 1957.

Unckless, Leslie. How to Find Manufacturing Costs and Selling Costs. Detroit: Modern Methods Publishing Company, 1909.

Urofsky, Melvin I., and Levy, David W., eds. Letters of Louis D. Brandeis, Vol. II. Albany, N.Y.: State University of New York Press, 1972.

Vance, Lawrence, and Taussig, Russell A. Accounting Principles and Control. New York: Holt, Rinehart and Winston, 1972.

Walton, Seymour, and Gilman, Stephen W. Auditing and Cost Accounts. New York: Alexander Hamilton Institute, 1911.

Weber, Charles. The Evolution of Direct Costing. Urbana, Illinois: Center for International Education and Research in Accounting, 1966.

Weber, Karl, Dr. Amerikanische Standardkostenrechung: Ein Uberlick. Verlag P.G. Keller -- Winterthur, 1960. (American Cost Accounting: An Overview. Winterthur: P.G. Keller, 1960.)

Webner, Frank Erastus. Factory Costs. New York: Ronald Press, 1911.

Wildman, John Raymond. Cost Accounting. New York: Accountancy Publishing Company, 1911.

Wren, Daniel A. The Evolution of Management Thought. New York: The Ronald Press Company, 1972.

Periodicals

Adams, C.W. "The Differential Piece Rate." American Machinist, Vol. XXXIV (January 5, 1911), pp. 18-19.

"Advanced Bookkeeping and Accounts Paper No. 3." Journal of Accountancy, Vol. XII, No. 6 (October, 1911), p. 480.

Aitken, Hugh G.J. review of Scientific Management and the Unions 1900-1932: A Historical Analysis, by Milton J. Nadworny, in Business History Review, Vol. XXX, No. 1 (March, 1956), p. 101.

Alford, L.P. "Scientific Management in Use." American Machinist, Vol. XXXVI, No. 14 (April 4, 1912), pp. 548-52.

Allingham, Henry W. "Determination of Standards in Scientific Management." Accountant, April 26, 1919, pp. 345-52.

American Accounting Association. "Report of the Committee on Accounting History." The Accounting Review, Supplement to Vol. XLV, 1970, pp. 53-64.

American History Committee for the 1938 International Management Congress. "History of Scientific Management in America." Mechanical Engineering, September, 1939, pp. 671-75.

Anderson, W.P. "Cost Keeping for Reinforced Concrete Buildings." Engineering Magazine, Vol. XLV (April, 1913), pp. 34-49.

Annett, C.B., and Cunningham, C.F. "Textile Cost Accounting: A Brief Treatise on its Purpose and Application." Transactions of the American Society of Mechanical Engineers,[1] Vol. XXXV, 1913, pp. 555-65.

---

[1]Referred to in future as Trans. ASME.

Armstrong, George W. "Cost Accounting--The Key to Cost Control." Railway Mechanical Engineer, June, 1920, pp. 374-79.

Arnold, Horace L. "Cost Finding Methods for Moderate Sized Shops." Engineering Magazine, Vol. XXIV (December, 1902), pp. 385-95.

________. "The Expense Account of the Machine Shop." Engineering Magazine, Vol. XX (December, 1900), pp. 365-72.

Atkinson, Henry. "Incentives to Efficiency Under Scientific Management." Accountant, July 26, August 2, 1919, pp. 94-96, 105-112.

Austin, Sir Herbert. "General Value of Cost Control and Organization in the Factory." Accountant, June 19, 1920, pp. 721-24.

Babcock, George De A. "Results of Scientific Management." American Machinist, Vol. XL, No. 25, pp. 1063-68.

Bancroft, Wilfred. "New Factory Cost Accounting System." American Machinist, July 24, 1902, pp. 1048-52.

Barber, Robert Nodes. "Works Accounting." Accountant, April 3, 1909, pp. 470-78.

Barnes, Fred Asa. "Cost Keeping and Management." Cornell Civil Engineer, 1915, pp. 434-45.

Barth, C.G. "Betterment of Machine Tool Operation by Scientific Metal Cutting." Engineering Magazine, Vol. XLII, pp. 586-92.

Bentley, H.C. "A Problem in the Distribution of Expense Burden." Journal of Accountancy, Vol. XVI, No. 1 (July, 1913), pp. 25-50.

________. "A Problem in the Distribution of Expense Burden." Journal of Accountancy, Vol. XVI, No. 3 (September, 1913), pp. 175-209.

Binsse, Henry Leon. "A Short Way to Keep Time and Cost." Trans. ASME, Vol. IX, 1887, pp. 380-89.

Bird, William W. "A Foundry Cost and Accounting System." Trans. ASME, Vol. XL, 1918, pp. 67-84.

Bosher, Lewis H. "Controlling Accounts in Cost Accounting." Journal of Accountancy, June, 1912, pp. 405-19.

Boyd, J.H.H. "Costing in Relation to Scientific Management." Accountant, July 12, 1919, pp. 33-40.

________. "Costing in Relation to Scientific Management." Electrician, August 28, 1919, pp. 171-72.

Brandeis, Louis D. "New Conception of Industrial Efficiency." Journal of Accountancy, May, 1911, pp. 35-43.

Brown, W.V. "Scientific Management: A list of References in the New York Public Library." New York (City) Public Library Bulletin, January, February, 1917, pp. 19-43, 83-136.

Bunnell, Sterling H. "Are Profits a Proper Measure of Efficiency?" The Iron Age, December 5, 1912, pp. 1318-19.

________. "Cost Accounting: What the Federal Trade Commission is Doing to Promote Business Efficiency." Painters Magazine, Vol. XLIII (September, 1916), pp. 476-80.

________. "Cost-Keeping and Efficiency in Engineering." Canadian Engineer, March 9, 1916, pp. 329-32.

________. "Expense Burden: Its Incidence and Distribution." Trans. ASME, Vol. XXXIII, 1911, pp. 535-59.

________. "Proper Use of Cost Keeping System." Cassiers Magazine, August, 1908, pp. 300-303.

Burton, Francis George. "Cost Accounts." Accountant, February 24, 1912, pp. 324-31.

Butterworth, J.F. "Modern Methods in Industry." Accountant, March 6, 1920, pp. 276-82.

Chandler, Alfred D. "The Beginnings of 'Big Business' in American Industry." Business History Review, Winter, 1959, pp. 1-31.

Church, Alexander Hamilton. "Cost and Time Keeping Outfit of the Taylor System." American Machinist, Vol. XXIX (December 13, 1906), pp. 761-63.

________. "The Meaning of Commercial Organization." Engineering Magazine, Vol. XX, No. 3 (December, 1900), pp. 391-98.

________. "The Meaning of Scientific Management." Engineering Magazine, Vol. XLI (April, 1911), pp. 97-101.

________. "The Proper Distribution of Establishment Charges." (Series of 6 articles) Engineering Magazine, 1901, pp. 508-17, 726-34, 904-12, 1902, pp. 31-40, 231-40, 367-76.

Clark, E.A. "How we Keep Costs in Our 75 Man Plant." Factory, October, 1916, pp. 405-408.

Cleveland, F.A. "The Scope of the Profession of Accountancy." The Journal of Accountancy, Vol. 1, No. 1 (November, 1905), pp. 40-56.

Coes, Harold V. "Rehabilitation of Existing Plants as a Factor in Production Costs." Engineering Magazine, June, 1915, pp. 357-71.

Cole, William Morse. "Accounting Methods for Determining Costs and Prices." American Economics Association Bulletin, April, 1911, pp. 124-35.

________. "The Rise of Accountancy." Journal of Accountancy, Vol. VII, No. 4 (February, 1909), pp. 295-96.

Cooley, Morgan L. "Successful Accountancy." Journal of Accountancy, Vol. VII, No. 4 (February, 1909), pp. 297-302.

Copley, Frank Barkley. "Frederick W. Taylor, Revolutionist." The Outlook, September 1, 1915, pp. 41-48.

Craggs, G. Sommerville. "Manufacturing Costs." Accountant, June 5, 1915, pp. 756-66.

Crossman, Paul. "The Genesis of Cost Control." Accounting Review, Vol. XXVIII, October, 1953, pp. 522-27.

Cudworth, Alfred James. "Some Notes on Cost Accounts." Accountant, April 18, 1896, pp. 312-19.

Dale, Ernest, and Meloy, Charles. "Hamilton McFarland Barksdale and the DuPont Contributions to Scientific Management." Business History Review, Vol. XXXVI, Summer, 1962, pp. 127-52.

"Dangerous Labor Legislation Now Before Congress--A Call for Prompt Action." editorial in Engineering Magazine, Vol. LI, No. 1 (April, 1916), pp. 1-11.

Darnell, R.W. "Standards as a Means of Reducing Costs." National Association of Cost Accountants Yearbook, N.Y.C., 1922, pp. 192-216.

"Definitions of Cost, Unit Cost, Direct and Indirect Cost, and Overhead Cost." Engineering and Contracting, Vol. XLVII, No. 9 (February 28, 1917), pp. 196-97.

Dickinson, A. Lowes. "Accounting Practice and Procedure--VI. Receivers and Assignees in Bankruptcy and Plans of Reorganization." Journal of Accountancy, Vol. VII, No. 2 (December, 1908), pp. 96-100.

Diemer, Hugo. "Cost Finding Methods for Moderate Sized Shops." Engineering Magazine, Vol. XXIV (January, 1903), pp. 577-89.

________. "Industrial Management." Journal of Accountancy, Vol. III, No. 2 (December, 1906), pp. 272-78.

Dodge, James M. "A History of the Introduction of a System of Shop Management." Trans. ASME, Vol. XXVII, 1906, pp. 720-29.

Dolge, William. "The Antonym in Accounting." The Journal of Accountancy, Vol. IX, No. 6 (April, 1910), p. 455.

Duncan, James. "Efficiency." Journal of Accountancy, Vol. XII, No. 1 (May, 1911), pp. 26-34.

Duncan, John C. "Methods of Determining the Efficiency of Labor." The Journal of Accountancy, Vol. I, No. 4 (February, 1906), pp. 301-309.

Dunlap, John. "The Literature of Industrial Management: Historical Events in the Development of a New Science." Engineering Magazine, Vol. IL (May, 1915), pp. 163-66.

Edwards, John R. "The Fetishism of Scientific Management." Journal of the American Society of Naval Engineers, Vol. XXIV, No. 2 (May, 1912).

Eggleston, D. Carl. "Evolution of the Machine Unit System at the Modern Electric Company." Journal of Accountancy, Vol. XII, No. 1 (May, 1911), pp. 44-57.

________. "A Municipal Cost System." The Journal of Accountancy, Vol. XII, No. 8 (December, 1911), pp. 573-87.

________. "Series of Articles about Factory Cost Accounting." Businessman's Magazine, November, December, 1907, January, 1908, pp. 81-84, 78-82, 95-100.

________. "A System of Factory Cost Accounting." The Journal of Accountancy, Vol. III, No. 2 (December, 1906), pp. 115-22.

Eilbirt, Henry. "The Development of Personnel Management in the United States." Business History Review, Vol. XXXIII, No. 3 (1959), pp. 345-64.

Elbourne, Edward T. "Functions of Factory Accounts." Accountant, May 3, 1919, pp. 361-65.

Emerson, Harrington. "Fundamental Truth of Scientific Management." Journal of Accountancy, Vol. XII, No. 1 (May, 1911), pp. 17-25.

________. "Reliable, Immediate, Adequate, and Permanent Records." Engineering Magazine, January, 1911, pp. 495-506.

________. "The Twelve Principles of Efficiency." Engineering Magazine, January, 1911, pp. 496-506.

Evans, Holden A. "Distribution of Indirect Costs." American Machinist, Vol. XXXIII (December 22, 1910), pp. 1158-61.

________. "The Various Elements of Cost." American Machinist, Vol. XXXIII (December 8, 1910), pp. 1050-54.

Fagan, James O. "The Dream of Scientific Management on Railroads." The Journal of Accountancy, Vol. XII, No. 1 (May, 1911), pp. 1-16.

Falk, Henry J. "The Importance of Systems for Garages." The Journal of Accountancy, Vol. XII, No. 6 (October, 1911), pp. 410-14.

Falk, Myron S. "A System of Cost Keeping." Transactions of the American Society of Civil Engineers, Vol. LXIV, 1909, pp. 401-40.

Fells, John M. "Conference on Scientific Costing: Cost Accountancy: Its Evolution and Its Trend." Accountant, June 28, 1919, pp. 548-52.

________. "Some Principles Governing the Ascertainment of Cost." Business Organization and Management, July, 1920, pp. 425-30.

Fish. E.H. "What Constitutes Overhead." The Engineering Magazine, July, 1915, pp. 488-97.

Fletcher, F. Richmond. "Standards as a Means of Reducing Costs." in National Association of Cost Accountants Yearbook 1922 and Proceedings of the Third International Cost Conference. New York: National Association of Cost Accountants, 1922, pp. 157-91.

Forbes, Frederick. "Brandeis Tells How U.S. Railroads can Save $1,000,000 a Day." Philadelphia North American, November 22, 1910.

Fowler, George L. "Estimating the Cost of Foundry Work." Trans. ASME, Vol. IX, 1887, pp. 390-97.

Franklin, Benjamin A. "Building a Cost System." Engineering Magazine, December, 1913, pp. 356-64.

________. "Cost Methods That Give the Executive Control of His Business." Engineering Magazine, pp. 577-85.

________. "Experiences in Efficiency." Engineering Magazine, December, 1913, pp. 356-64.

Gaines, Morrell W. "Tabulating Machine Cost Accounting for Factories of Diversified Product." Engineering Magazine, Vol. XXX (December, 1905), pp. 364-73.

Galloway, Lee, ed. Review of Cost-Keeping for Manufacturing Plants, by Sterling H. Bunnell. Review of Workshop Costs, Engineers and Manufacturers, by Sinclair Pearn and Frank Pearn. Journal of Accountancy, Vol. XII, No. 4 (August, 1911), pp. 306-09.

________. Review of How to Find Manufacturing Costs and Selling Costs, by Leslie Unckless. Journal of Accountancy, Vol. XII, No. 4 (August, 1911), pp. 309-10.

________. Review of The Management of Engineering Workshops, by Arthur A. Barker. Journal of Accountancy, Vol. XII, No. 4 (August, 1911), pp. 303-04.

________. Review of Methods of the Santa Fe, by Charles Buxton Goings. Journal of Accountancy, Vol. XII, No. 2 (June, 1911), p. 141.

_______. Review of _Principles of Industrial Engineering_, by Charles Buxton Goings. Review of _Factory Organization and Administration_, by Hugo Diemer. _Journal of Accountancy_, Vol. XII, No. 5 (September, 1911), pp. 382-87.

_______. Review of _The Principles of Scientific Management_, by Frederick W. Taylor. _Journal of Accountancy_, Vol. XIII, No. 5 (May, 1912), pp. 385-86.

_______. Review of _Scientific Management_, by Louis D. Brandeis. Review of _Work, Wages, and Profits_, by H.L. Gantt. Review of _Production Factors in Cost Accounting and Works Management_, by A. Hamilton Church. _Journal of Accountancy_, Vol. XII, No. 1 (May, 1911), pp. 69-74.

_______. Review of _Twelve Principles of Efficiency_, by Harrington Emerson. Review of _Efficiency as a Basis for Operations and Wages_, by Harrington Emerson. _Journal of Accountancy_, Vol. XIII, No. 4 (April, 1912).

Gantt, H.L. "A Practical Application of Scientific Management." _Engineering Magazine_, Vol. XLI, No. 1, pp. 1-22.

_______. "Production and Sales." _Engineering Magazine_, January, 1916, pp. 593-600.

_______. "The Relation Between Costs and Production." _The Gas Engine_, Vol. XVIII (October, 1916), pp. 521-24.

_______. "The Relation Between Production and Costs." _Trans. ASME_, Vol. XXXVII (1915), pp. 109-17.

_______. "The Relation Between Production and Costs: Discussion." _Trans. ASME_, Vol. XXXVII (1915), pp. 117-28.

Garry, H. Stanley. "Factory Costs." _The Accountant_, July 25, 1903, pp. 954-61.

Gilbreth, F.B. "Theory at Work." _Journal of Accountancy_, July, 1911, pp. 195-200.

Godfrey, Stuart C. "Cost Keeping and Efficiency in Works of the Engineer Department." _United States Engineer Corps Professional Memoirs_, Vol. VIII (January/February, 1916), pp. 1-30.

Golden, John. "The Attitude of Organized Labor." The Journal of Accountancy, Vol. XII, No. 3 (July, 1911), pp. 189-94.

Gunn, James Newton. "Cost Keeping: A Subject of Fundamental Importance." Engineering Magazine, Vol. XX (January, 1901), pp. 703-08.

Halsey, F.A. "The Premium Plan of Paying for Labor." Trans. ASME, Vol. XII (1891), pp. 755-80.

Hamburger, Richard A. "Sources of Accounting History." An appendix to the report of the American Accounting Association's Committee on Accounting History. Accounting Review, Supplement to Vol. XLV (1970), p. 64.

Harrington, C.A. "The Relation of Detailed Planning and the Cost of Production." Engineering Magazine, June, 1913, pp. 353-58.

Harrison, G. Charter. "Scientific Basis for Cost Accounting." Industrial Management, March, 1920, pp. 237-42.

________. "What is Wrong With Cost Accounting?" Management Engineering, Vol. I, No. 1 (July, 1921), pp. 29-32.

Hauer, Daniel J. "How a Cost Keeping System Should be Devised and Used." The Contractor, Vol. XXIII (April, 1916), pp. 29-31.

Hays, Samuel P. "The Politics of Reform in Municipal Government in the Progressive Era." Pacific Northwest Quarterly, October, 1964, pp. 157-69.

Hill, George W. "A Unit Time-Card and Pay Roll System." Electrical Review and Western Electrician, Vol. LXVIII (April 15, 1916), pp. 681-83.

Hiller, August. "Cost Systematizing." Journal of Accountancy, Vol. XVI, No. 6 (December, 1913), pp. 435-39.

Hutchins, F. Lincoln. "A Practical Plan for Standardizing Railroad Records." Engineering Magazine, Vol. XLV (August, 1913), pp. 664-68.

Jackson, A.C.; Smith, A.; and Towne, H.R. "Axioms Concerning Manufacturing Costs." Trans. ASME, April, 1913.

Jenks, Leland H. "Early Phases of the Management Movement." Administrative Science Quarterly, Vol. V (December, 1960), pp. 421-49.

Johnson, Joseph French, ed. "Accountancy and Economics." Journal of Accountancy, Vol. VI, No. 2 (June, 1908), p. 140.

________. "Conference on Scientific Management." Journal of Accountancy, Vol. XII, No. 2 (June, 1911), pp. 134-35.

________. "Foundry Costs." Journal of Accountancy, Vol. VI, No. 3 (July, 1908), pp. 217-18.

________. "Efficiency and Railroad Management." The Journal of Accountancy, Vol. XI, No. 3 (January, 1911), pp. 218-19.

________. "An Explanation and an Invitation." Journal of Accountancy, Vol. V, No. 5 (September, 1911), pp. 377-78.

________. "Scientific Business Management." The Journal of Accountancy, Vol. XII, No. 1 (May, 1911), pp. 58-59.

Kolker, Kenneth K. "The Changing Status of the Foreman." Bulletin of the Business Historical Society, Vol. XXIII, No. 3 (June, 1948), pp. 84-101.

Lane, H.M. "A Method of Determining Selling Price." Trans. ASME, Vol. XVIII (1896), pp. 221-29.

________. "A Method of Shop Accounting to Determine Shop Cost and Minimum Selling Price." Trans. ASME, Vol. XVIII (1897), pp. 892-900.

Lauer, Conrad N. "Importance of Cost Keeping to the Manufacturer." Annals of the American Academy of Political and Social Science, November, 1903, pp. 459-69.

Le Rossignol, James Edward. "The Relation Between Accountancy and Economics." The Journal of Accountancy, Vol. IX, No. 2 (December, 1909), pp. 81-88.

Lewis, Wilfred. "Efficiency Methods of the Tabor Manufacturing Company." Iron Age, Vol. LXXXVII (April 13, 1911), pp. 902-03.

Litterer, Joseph A. "Alexander Hamilton Church and the Development of Modern Management." Business History Review, Vol. XXXV, No. 2 (1961), pp. 211-25.

________. "Systematic Management: Design for Organizational Recoupling in American Manufacturing Firms." Business History Review, Vol. XXXVII, No. 4 (1963), pp. 369-91.

Littleton, A.C. "Socialized Accounts." Accounting Review, Vol. VIII, No. 4 (December, 1933), pp. 270-71.

Logan, James. "The Importance of Scientific Accounting." The Journal of Accountancy, Vol. VI, No. 4 (August, 1908), pp. 276-79.

Longmuir, Percy. "Recording the Interpreting Foundry Costs." The Engineering Magazine, September, 1902, pp. 887-94.

Lybrand, William M. "The Accounting of Industrial Enterprises, Part III. Depreciation." Journal of Accountancy, Vol. VII, No. 3 (January, 1909), pp. 224-36.

McHenry, William E. "Is your Cost System Scientific." Engineering Magazine, Vol. LI (August, 1916), pp. 678-86.

Mason, J.K. "Synthetic Costs." Engineering Magazine, Vol. LII (October, 1916), pp. 63-66.

Massey, James R. "Relationship of Costing to Management." Accountant, July 5, 1919, pp. 12-17.

Maxwell, F. Crofton. "Scientific Presentation of Costs." Accounting and Commerce, December, 1919, January, 1920, pp. 213-15, 235-42.

Metcalfe, Henry. "The Shop Order System of Accounts." Trans. ASME, Vol. VII (1886), pp. 440-68, 475-88.

Millener, C.A. "Evolution of Cost Accounts." Business, July, August, September, October, November, 1895, pp. 266-69, 302-04, 332-36, 361-62, 399-400.

Miller. Fred J. "Scientific Management: Its Installation and Operation." Efficiency Society Journal, Vol. V (March, 1916), pp. 118-36.

Miller, H.C. "Applying Efficiency Standards in Central Station Accounting." Journal of Accountancy, Vol. XVI, No. 6 (December, 1913), pp. 432-34.

Miller W.M.S. "Errors and Difficulties in Manufacturing Costs." Engineering Magazine, February, 1909, pp. 825-32.

Murdoch, Andrew A. "The Proper Treatment of Machine Costs--A Criticism and A Theory." The Journal of Accountancy, Vol. III, No. s (December, 1906), pp. 123-30.

Murphy, Mary E. "Notes on Accounting History." Accounting Research, January, 1950, pp. 275-80.

Nadworny, Milton J. "Frederick Taylor and Frank Gilbreth: Competition in Scientific Management." Business History Review, Vol. XXXI (1957), pp. 23-34.

Nav, Carl H. "Accounting as a Basis for and a Measure of Efficiency in Business." Journal of Accountancy, Vol. XV, No. 3 (March, 1913), pp. 143-56.

Nicholl, John S. "A Scientific Cost Keeping System for Reinforced Concrete." Engineering Magazine, Vol. XLIV (January, 1913), pp. 511-25.

Norris, H.M. "An Accurate Cost Keeping System." Trans. ASME, Vol. XIX (1897-1898), pp. 387-414.

Orcutt, H.F. "Machine Shop Management in Europe and America." The Engineering Magazine, 1899, pp. 549-55, 703-10, 921-31.

Plumpton, Thomas. "Manufacturing Costs." Accountant, March 26, 1892, pp. 267-71.

Poor, Henry. "Railroad Share List, Including Mileage, Rolling Stock, Etc." American Railroad Journal, Vol. XXIX (January 14, 1856), pp. 6-7.

Porter, Harry F. "Cost Keeping the Basis of Prosperity." Engineering Magazine, Vol. LI, No. 3 (June, 1916), pp. 325-32.

Powell, Paul R. "Cost Keeping in Small Factories." Engineering Magazine, Vol. XL (October, 1910), pp. 31-37.

Raymond, Robert H. "History of the Flexible Budget." Management Accounting, Vol. XLVII, No. 12 (August, 1966), pp. 9-15.

Reckitt, Ernest. "Some Principles of Cost Accounting." The Journal of Accountancy, Vol. VII, No. 4 (February, 1909), pp. 356-67.

Redding, C.J. "A Simple System of Recording Costs." Engineering Magazine, Vol. XXXIV (February, 1908), pp. 781-92.

Richards, Frank. "Is Anything the Matter with Piece Work?: Discussion." Trans. ASME, Vol. XXV (1903), pp. 73-92.

Rogers, Della Mae. "Development of the Modern Business Budget." Journal of Accountancy, Vol. LIII, No. 3 (March, 1932), pp. 186-205.

Roland, Henry. "Cost-Keeping Methods in Machine Shop and Foundry." Engineering Magazine, Vol. XIV (1897-1898), pp. 56-63, 225-38, 464-72, 626-34.

________. "An Effective System of Finding and Keeping Shop Costs." Engineering Magazine, Vol. XV (1898), pp. 77-86, 241-48, 395-400, 610-20, 749-58, 1000-1016.

Runnells, John S., and Husband, J. "What a New System of Management Did for Us." System, July, 1916, pp. 78-87.

Scovell, Clinton Homer. "Cost Accounting Practice with Special Reference to Machine Hour Rate." Journal of Accountancy, January, 1914, pp. 13-27.

________. "Determination of Foundry Costs." Iron Age, Vol. XCVIII (October 5, 1916), pp. 764-65.

________. "Finding Out About Factory Profits." Industrial Engineering and Engineering Digest, Vol. XIV, No. 6 (June, 1914), pp. 246-50.

Searle, H.F. "The Premium System for the Payment of Wages." The Journal of Accountancy, Vol. IX, No. 5 (March, 1910), pp. 321-39.

Secretary of the Navy. Annual Report, reprinted in part entitled "Cost Accounting in the Navy." Journal of Accountancy, Vol. IX, No. 4 (February, 1910), pp. 300-301.

Sells, Elijah W. "Cost Accounting." The Journal of Accountancy, Vol. IX, No. 3 (January, 1910), pp. 171-76.

Shaw, A. J. "Machine Shop Time and Cost Accounts." American Machinist, April 3, 1886, pp. 3-4.

Sinclair, Upton. "The Principles of Scientific Management; A Criticism and an answer by F.W. Taylor." American Magazine, March, 1911.

Smith, Oberlin. "System in Machine Shops." American Machinist, October 31, 1885, pp. 1-2.

Steele, F.R. Carnegie. "The Development of Systems of Control." Journal of Accountancy, Vol. XVI, No. 4 (October, 1913), pp. 280-90.

Sterling, F.W. "The Successful Operation of a System of Scientific Management." Journal of the American Society of Naval Engineers, Vol. XXIV, p. 167.

Sturgess, John. "A Simple Cost System for Complex Situations." Engineering Magazine, Vol. XXXVI (March, 1909), pp. 940-48.

Suffern, Edward L. "Railway Efficiency." The Journal of Accountancy, Vol. II, No. 3 (January, 1911), pp. 221-22. (Reprinted from New York Times, December 4, 1910.)

Suffern, Ernest S. "The Man in the Ranks: How He Benefits Through Scientific Management." The Journal of Accountancy, Vol. XII, No. 8 (December, 1911), pp. 565-72.

Tarbell, Ida M. "Making the Most of Men." Bulletin of the Taylor Society, Vol. X, No. 1 (February, 1925), pp. 80-81.

Tardy, W.B. "Scientific Management and Efficiency in the United States Navy." Engineering Magazine, Vol. XLI, No. 4 (July, 1911), pp. 545-68.

Taylor, F.W. "On the Art of Cutting Metals." Trans. ASME, Vol. XXVIII, No. 1119 (December, 1906), pp. 31-58.

________. "A Piece Rate System Being a Step Toward Partial Solution of the Labor Problem." Trans. ASME, Vol. XVI (1895), pp. 856-903.

________. "Principles and Methods of Scientific Management." Journal of Accountancy, June, July, 1911, pp. 117-24, 181-88.

Teichmann, Max. "A Sketch of Accountancy." The Journal of Accountancy, Vol. XIII, No. 6 (June, 1912), pp. 420-30.

Theiss, Edwin L. "The Beginnings of Business Budgeting." Accounting Review, Vol. XII, No. 1 (March, 1937), pp. 43-55.

Thompson, C. Bertrand. "Taking Factory Costs Apart." Magazine of Business, February, 1913, pp. 131-37.

Thompson, Sanford E.; Lichtner, William O.; Hall, Keppele; and Guild, Henry J. "Development of Scientific Methods of Management in a Manufacturing Plant." Trans. ASME, Vol. XXXIX (1917), pp. 123-72.

Towne, Henry R. "Axioms Concerning Manufacturing Costs." Trans. ASME, December, 1912, pp. 1945-57.

________. "Axioms Concerning Manufacturing Costs." Trans. ASME, Vol. XXXIV (1912), pp. 1111-23.

________. "Axioms Concerning Manufacturing Costs: Discussion." Trans. ASME, Vol. XXXIV (1912), pp. 1123-29.

________. "The Engineer as an Economist." Trans. ASME, Vol. VII (1885-1886), pp. 428-33.

________. "The General Principles of Organization Applied to an Individual Manufacturing Establishment." Transactions of the Efficiency Society, Vol. 1, No. 2, pp. 77-83.

Vedder, H.C.M. "Cost Accounting: An Exposition of its Theories and Principles." Accountant, November 11, 1905, pp. 545-51.

Webner, Frank E. "A Treatise on Cost Finding." Industrial Engineering and The Engineering Digest, May, 1912, pp. 357-62.

Whitmore, John. "Factory Accounting as Applied to Machine Shops, Part I." The Journal of Accountancy, Vol. II, No. 4 (August, 1906), pp. 248-58.

________. "Factory Accounting as Applied to Machine Shops, Part II." The Journal of Accountancy, Vol. II, No. 5 (September, 1906), pp. 345-57.

________. "Factory Accounting as Applied to Machine Shops, Part III." The Journal of Accountancy, Vol. II, No. 6 (October, 1906), pp. 430-41.

________. "Factory Accounting as Applied to Machine Shops, Part IV." The Journal of Accountancy, Vol. III, No. 1 (November, 1906), pp. 20-31.

________. "Factory Accounting as Applied to Machine Shops, Part V." The Journal of Accountancy, Vol. III, No. 2 (December, 1906), pp. 106-14.

________. "Factory Accounting as Applied to Machine Shops, Part VI." The Journal of Accountancy, Vol. III, No. 3 (January, 1907), pp. 211-18.

________. "Shoe Factory Cost Accounts." Journal of Accountancy, Vol. VI, No. 1 (May, 1908), pp. 12-25.

________. "Some Details of Machine Shop Cost Accounts." The Journal of Accountancy, Vol. III, No. 4 (February, 1907), pp. 294-96.

Wildman, John R. Review of Efficiency as a Basis for Operation and Wages, by Harrington Emerson. The Journal of Accountancy, Vol. IX, No. 2 (December, 1909), pp. 145-47.

________. Review of Factory Costs, by Frank E. Webner. The Journal of Accountancy, Vol. XIII, No. 1 (January, 1912), pp. 68-70.

Letters

Letter from Carl Barth, Philadelphia, March 18, 1907, to Francis Taylor, V.P. Yale & Towne Mfg. Company.

Letter from Wm. D. Basley to F.W. Taylor, July 12, 1893. Found in Frederick Winslow Taylor Collection, Stevens Institute of Technology, Hoboken, New Jersey.

Letter from R.H. Durham, Bethlehem Steel Company to F.W. Taylor, South Bethlehem, Pa., January 6, 1900.

Letter from H.K. Hathaway to Frank B. Copley, April 18, 1921. Found in Frederick Winslow Taylor Collection, Stevens Institute of Technology, Hoboken, New Jersey.

Letter from R.H. Jones, Bethlehem Iron Company to F.W. Taylor, August 9, 1899.

Letter from Robert Linderman, President of Bethlehem Iron Company, South Bethlehem, Pa., June 8, 1898 to F.W. Taylor.

Letter from Wilfred Lewis, President of Tabor Manufacturing Company, Philadelphia, Pa., to F.W. Taylor, February 10, 1911.

Letter from Wilfred Lewis, President of Tabor Manufacturing Company, Philadelphia, Pa., to F.W. Taylor, February 13, 1911.

Letter from Wilfred Lewis, President of Tabor Manufacturing Company, Philadelphia, Pa., to F.W. Taylor, May 1, 1911.

Letter from F.W. Taylor, Fitchburg, Mass., to Robert Linderman, President of Bethlehem Iron Company, South Bethlehem, Pa., January 4, 1898.

Letter from F.W. Taylor to Robert Linderman, President of Bethlehem Iron Company, South Bethlehem, Pa., August 8, 1898.

Letter from F.W. Taylor to Robert Linderman, President of Bethlehem Iron Company, South Bethlehem, Pa., February 27, 1899.

Letter from F.W. Taylor to Robert Linderman, President of Bethlehem Steel Company, South Bethlehem, Pa., October 5, 1899.

Letter from F.W. Taylor to Robert Linderman, South Bethlehem, Pa., April 4, 1901.

Letter from F.W. Taylor, Consulting Engineer, South Bethlehem, Pa., to Joseph Wharton, April 4, 1901.

Letter from F.W. Taylor to Richard W. Yerkes, Sales Manager, Link Belt Company, May 28, 1908.

Letter from L.S. Wingby, Camden Iron Works, Camden, New Jersey, to F.W. Taylor, April 16, 1891.

Letter from Richard W. Yerkes, Sales Manager, Link Belt Company, Nicetown, Pa., May 27, 1908.

Unpublished Materials

Abyanker, B. "F.W. Taylor--Personal Life, An Institution, and The Ambiguity of Taylor's Position in the History of Industrial Society." Unpublished manuscript, F.W. Taylor Collection, Stevens Institute of Technology, Hoboken, New Jersey, 1960.

Barth, Carl. "Approval of Bills by the Auditor." Unpublished material from F.W. Taylor Collection, Stevens Institute of Technology, Hoboken, New Jersey.

________. "A Brief Description of the Eight Large Gray Canvas Covered Books of Taylor Memorabilia." Unpublished Manuscript, F.W. Taylor Collection, Stevens Institute of Technology, Hoboken, New Jersey, 1933.

________. "Cost System." Unpublished material from F.W. Taylor Collection, Stevens Institute of Technology, Hoboken, New Jersey.

________. "Expense Sheet Form." Unpublished material from F.W. Taylor Collection, Stevens Institute of Technology, Hoboken, New Jersey.

Bethlehem Iron Company. "Sheet for Determining Relative Cost Numbers." Form, unpublished material, F.W. Taylor Collection, Stevens Institute of Technology, Hoboken, New Jersey, 1899.

Chatfield, Michael. "Accounting Problems of the Industrial Corporation." Unpublished work.

Eastern Manufacturing Company. "Standing Order No. 26, Inspector of Cost." Unpublished material from F.W. Taylor Collection, Stevens Institute of Technology, Hoboken, New Jersey, August 30, 1915.

Gantt, H.L. "Report on the System of Task Work With a Premium as Now in Operation in No. 2 Machine Shop with an Explanation of the Principles on Which it is Based." Unpublished report from F.W. Taylor Collection, Stevens Institute of Technology, Hoboken, New Jersey, May 13, 1901.

Midvale Steel Company. "Observations of Hand-Work on Machine Tools." Form, unpublished material from F.W. Taylor Collection, Stevens Institute of Technology, Hoboken, New Jersey, January 24, 1884.

________. "Rate Tables." Unpublished material from F.W. Taylor Collection, Stevens Institute of Technology, Hoboken, New Jersey, February 1, 1886.

Smith. A.L. "Cost of Emptying and Filling a Digester." Unpublished report of Manufacturers Investment Company, Appleton, Wisconsin, November 7, 1892. Found in the F.W. Taylor Collection, Stevens Institute of Technology, Hoboken, New Jersey.

The Steel Motor Company. "Cost of Motors, Parts of Motors, Controllers, Canopy Switches, etc." Form, unpublished material from F.W. Taylor Collection, Stevens Institute of Technology, Hoboken, New Jersey, 189_.

________. "Detailed cost of Controllers, Gears, Trolleys, Pinions, Gear Casings and Suspensions." Form, unpublished material from F.W. Taylor Collection, Stevens Institute of Technology, Hoboken, New Jersey, 189_.

________. "Income Account." Form, unpublished material from F.W. Taylor Collection, Stevens Institute of Technology, Hoboken, New Jersey, 189_.

Taylor, F.W. "Bookkeeping Under the Taylor System." Unpublished manuscript found in the Frederick Winslow Taylor Collection, Stevens Institute of Technology, Hoboken, New Jersey, 1893.

________. "Cost Keeping Under the Taylor System of Shop Management." Unpublished manuscript found in the Frederick Winslow Taylor Collection, Stevens Institute of Technology, Hoboken, New Jersey.

________. "Description of Sellers Method of Determining Costs at Wm. Sellers and Company." Unpublished manuscript found in F.W. Taylor Collection, Stevens Institute of Technology, Hoboken, New Jersey.

________. "System of Book Keeping and Returns." Unpublished manuscript found in F.W. Taylor Collection, Stevens Institute of Technology, Hoboken, New Jersey.

Thorne, Joe Allen. "The Influence of Federal Income Taxation on Selected Aspects of Accounting Practices and Reports." Unpublished Ph.D. dissertation, University of Alabama, 1967.

Other

Amos Tuck School Conference. *Addresses and Discussions at the Conference on Scientific Management*. October 12-14, 1911. Hanover, N.H.: Amos Tuck School of Administration and Finance, Dartmouth College, 1912.

Meyer, H.B., compiler. "Select list of references on scientific management and efficiency." Efficiency Number of Special Libraries, Library of Congress, May, 1913.

Tabor Manufacturing Company. President's Report for Year Ending December 31, 1910. Stevens Institute of Technology, F.W. Taylor Collection, Hoboken, New Jersey.

U.S. Congress. "The Taylor and Other Systems of Shop Management." Hearings before Special Committee of the House of Representatives, House Res. 90, October 1911 in 3 volumes.

U.S. Congressional Record. Senate debate on Dietrick Amendment. 63rd Congress, 3rd Session, February 23, 1915.

THE DEVELOPMENT OF CONTEMPORARY ACCOUNTING THOUGHT

An Arno Press Collection

Baldwin, H[arry] G[len]. **Accounting for Value As Well as Original Cost** *and* Castenholz, William B. **A Solution to the Appreciation Problem.** 2 Vols. in 1. 1927/1931

Baxter, William. **Collected Papers on Accounting.** 1978

Brief, Richard P., Ed. **Selections from Encyclopaedia of Accounting, 1903.** 1978

Broaker, Frank and Richard M. Chapman. **The American Accountants' Manual.** 1897

Canning, John B. **The Economics of Accountancy.** 1929

Chatfield, Michael, Ed. **The English View of Accountant's Duties and Responsibilities.** 1978

Cole, William Morse. **The Fundamentals of Accounting.** 1921

Congress of Accountants. **Official Record of the Proceedings of the Congress of Accountants.** 1904

Cronhelm, F[rederick] W[illiam]. **Double Entry by Single.** 1818

Davidson, Sidney. **The Plant Accounting Regulations of the Federal Power Commission.** 1952

De Paula, F[rederic] R[udolf] M[ackley]. **Developments in Accounting.** 1948

Epstein, Marc Jay. **The Effect of Scientific Management on the Development of the Standard Cost System** (Doctoral Dissertation, University of Oregon, 1973). 1978

Esquerré, Paul-Joseph. **The Applied Theory of Accounts.** 1914

Fitzgerald, A[dolf] A[lexander]. **Current Accounting Trends.** 1952

Garner, S. Paul and Marilynn Hughes, Eds. **Readings on Accounting Development.** 1978

Haskins, Charles Waldo. **Business Education and Accountancy.** 1904

Hein, Leonard William. **The British Companies Acts and the Practice of Accountancy 1844-1962** (Doctoral Dissertation, University of California, Los Angeles, 1962). 1978

Hendriksen, Eldon S. **Capital Expenditures in the Steel Industry, 1900 to 1953** (Doctoral Dissertation, University of California, Berkeley, 1956). 1978

Holmes, William, Linda H. Kistler and Louis S. Corsini. **Three Centuries of Accounting in Massachusetts.** 1978

Horngren, Charles T. **Implications for Accountants of the Uses of Financial Statements by Security Analysts** (Doctoral Dissertation, University of Chicago, 1955). 1978

Horrigan, James O., Ed. **Financial Ratio Analysis—An Historical Perspective.** 1978

Jones, [Edward Thomas]. **Jones's English System of Book-keeping.** 1796

Lamden, Charles William. **The Securities and Exchange Commission** (Doctoral Dissertation, University of California, Berkeley, 1949). 1978

Langer, Russell Davis. **Accounting As A Variable in Mergers** (Doctoral Dissertation, University of California, Berkeley, 1976). 1978

Lewis, J. Slater. **The Commercial Organisation of Factories.** 1896

Littleton, A[nanias] C[harles] and B[asil] S. Yamey, Eds. **Studies in the History of Accounting.** 1956

Mair, John. **Book-keeping Moderniz'd.** 1793

Mann, Helen Scott. **Charles Ezra Sprague.** 1931

Marsh, C[hristopher] C[olumbus]. **The Theory and Practice of Bank Book-keeping.** 1856

Mitchell, William. **A New and Complete System of Book-keeping by an Improved Method of Double Entry.** 1796

Montgomery, Robert H. **Fifty Years of Accountancy.** 1939

Moonitz, Maurice. **The Entity Theory of Consolidated Statements.** 1951

Moonitz, Maurice, Ed. **Three Contributions to the Development of Accounting Thought.** 1978

Murray, David. **Chapters in the History of Bookkeeping, Accountancy & Commercial Arithmetic.** 1930

Nicholson, J[erome] Lee. **Cost Accounting.** 1913

Paton, William Andrew and Russell Alger Stevenson. **Principles of Accounting.** 1918

Pixley, Francis W[illiam]. **The Profession of a Chartered Accountant and Other Lectures.** 1897

Preinreich, Gabriel A. D. **The Nature of Dividends.** 1935

Previts, Gary John, Ed. **Early 20th Century Developments in American Accounting Thought.** 1978

Ronen, Joshua and George H. Sorter. **Relevant Financial Statements.** 1978

Shenkir, William G., Ed. **Carman G. Blough: His Professional Career and Accounting Thought.** 1978

Simpson, Kemper. **Economics for the Accountant.** 1921

Sneed, Florence R. **Parallelism in Two Disciplines.** (M.A. Thesis, University of Texas, Arlington, 1974). 1978

Sorter, George H. **The Boundaries of the Accounting Universe** (Doctoral Dissertation, University of Chicago, 1963). 1978

Storey, Reed K[arl]. **Matching Revenues with Costs** (Doctoral Dissertation, University of California, Berkeley, 1958). 1978

Sweeney, Henry W[hitcomb]. **Stabilized Accounting.** 1936

Van de Linde, Gérard. **Reminiscences.** 1917

Vatter, William J[oseph]. **The Fund Theory of Accounting and Its Implications for Financial Reports.** 1947

Walker, R. G. **Consolidated Statements.** 1978

Webster, Norman E., Comp. **The American Association of Public Accountants.** 1954

Wells, M. C., Ed. **American Engineers' Contributions to Cost Accounting.** 1978

Worthington, Beresford. **Professional Accountants.** 1895

Yamey, Basil S. **Essays on the History of Accounting.** 1978

Yamey, Basil S., Ed. **The Historical Development of Accounting.** 1978

Yang, J[u] M[ei]. **Goodwill and Other Intangibles.** 1927

Zeff, Stephen Addam. **A Critical Examination of the Orientation Postulate in Accounting, with Particular Attention to its Historical Development** (Doctoral Dissertation, University of Michigan, 1961). 1978

Zeff, Stephen A., Ed. **Selected Dickinson Lectures in Accounting.** 1978